B-52 STRATOFORTRESS
UNITS IN COMBAT
1955-1973

SERIES EDITOR: TONY HOLMES

OSPREY COMBAT AIRCRAFT • 43

B-52 STRATOFORTRESS UNITS IN COMBAT 1955-1973

Jon Lake

OSPREY
PUBLISHING

Front cover

Bombs fall from a formation of B-52Fs of the 3960th Strategic Wing (SW) during an *Arc Light* bombing mission from Andersen AFB, Guam. The nearest B-52F was the aircraft flown by one Brig Gen Jimmy Stewart, USAF Reserve, who was then coming to the end of his USAF service. For his final two-week stint of active duty in 1966, Stewart had requested a combat assignment and had been duly sent on an inspection tour of Vietnam, where his 24-year-old stepson had recently been killed in action. During this brief period of active duty, Stewart participated in a bombing strike over Vietnam.

Although best known as a Hollywood actor, Stewart had also enjoyed a remarkable, and distinguished, military career. He had volunteered for active service in 1940, turning his back on what had been a lucrative profession as one of Hollywood's greatest stars. Stewart joined the USAAC in March 1941, a full nine months prior to the Japanese attack on Pearl Harbor and the United States' entry into the war. His determination allowed him to overcome the disadvantages of being too old and too skinny for military service, and he fought tirelessly to avoid propaganda assignments and official reluctance to place him in harm's way, striving to get an overseas combat duty assignment.

Stewart was finally assigned to the B-24-equipped 445th Bomb Group (BG) at Tibenham as operations officer, rising to command the 703rd BS before being transferred to 'turn around' the shattered 453rd BG. Stewart became a full colonel, and the 2nd Bomb Wing's chief of staff, in July 1944, and was promoted to Wing CO in the spring of 1945. He flew 20 bombing missions over Germany (against targets which included Brunswick, Bremen, Frankfurt, Schweinfurt, and Berlin), and was highly decorated. Despite resuming his acting career post-war, Stewart continued to take his Air Force Reserve duties extremely seriously, flying the B-47, B-52 and B-58.

Stewart is seen here flying B-52F 57-0149 (on its 36th combat sortie) on a daylight bombing mission against Viet Cong infiltrators (*Cover artwork by Mark Postlethwaite*)

First published in Great Britain in 2004 by Osprey Publishing
Elms Court, Chapel Way, Botley, Oxford, OX2 9LP

© 2004 Osprey Publishing Limited

ISBN 1 84176 607 0

Edited by Tony Holmes
Page design by Tony Truscott
Cover Artwork by Mark Postlethwaite
Aircraft Profiles and Line Artwork by Mark Styling
Index by Alan Thatcher
Origination by Grasmere Digital Imaging, Leeds, UK
Printed by Stamford Press PTE Ltd, Singapore

04 05 06 07 08   10 9 8 7 6 5 4 3 2 1

EDITOR'S NOTE
To make this best-selling series as authoritative as possible, the Editor would be interested in hearing from any individual who may have relevant photographs, documentation or first-hand experiences relating to the world's elite pilots, and their aircraft, of the various theatres of war. Any material used will be credited to its original source. Please write to Tony Holmes via e-mail at:
tony.holmes@osprey-jets.freeserve.co.uk

For a catalogue of all Osprey Publishing titles please contact us at:

Osprey Direct UK, PO Box 140, Wellingborough, Northants NN8 2FA, UK
E-mail: **info@ospreydirect.co.uk**

Osprey Direct USA, c/o MBI Publishing, 729 Prospect Ave, PO Box 1, Osceola, WI 54020, USA
E-mail: **info@ospreydirectusa.com**

CONTENTS

GENESIS OF THE B-52

Even as the aerospace industry celebrated the centenary of manned flight in 2003, the Boeing B-52 reached its own half-century. No other combat aircraft has enjoyed such a long frontline career with a major air force, and few have seen their missions and operational procedures change so dramatically.

Designed as the backbone of the United States' Cold War strategic nuclear deterrent, the B-52 spent the first years of its career standing alert, ready to go at a moment's notice, armed with deadly nuclear payloads. During the late 1950s and 1960s B-52s even maintained an airborne alert, patrolling close to the peripheries of the USSR, and ready to attack if ordered to do so.

The USA's nuclear alert forces 'stood down' on Presidential orders on 28 September 1991, and although the USAF's B-52s maintained a nuclear role, conventional bombing duties assumed a new significance, and were accorded the highest priority. The B-52's conventional capability had first been seriously exercised during the early 1960s, and was soon exploited in Southeast Asia.

During the Vietnam War, the B-52 was pressed into service to attack targets with ordinary high explosive, and it proved exceptionally effective and successful as a conventional bomber. The B-52 flew 126,615 sorties in Vietnam, dropping 2.63 million tons of bombs during its eight-year involvement. At the peak, there were more than 200 B-52s deployed, and the biggest mission of the war saw the despatch of no fewer than 129 aircraft!

Conventionally-armed B-52s subsequently went to war over Iraq during 1991's Operation *Desert Storm* (dropping another 25,700 tons

The XB-52 (the first Stratofortress built, but the second to fly) is seen here during early tests, with a line of B-50s parked behind it. The view from the 'fighter-type' cockpit canopy was superb in some directions, but poor in others, notably down over the aircraft's 'shoulders' (*Author's collection*)

of bombs in 1620 combat sorties), then again in Kosovo in 1999 and Afghanistan in 2001. Most recently, USAF B-52Hs were at war again during the landmark year of 2003, attacking targets in Iraq during Operation *Iraqi Freedom* – not bad for an aircraft which entered service to replace propeller-driven heavy bombers almost 50 years earlier.

During the late 1940s and early 1950s, when the B-52 took shape, the pace of technological development was extremely rapid, and few aircraft types served for more than a few years in the frontline. Under the USAF's original plans, the B-52 had been expected to be retired in 1964, with individual Stratofortresses serving for no longer than ten years. In the event, the B-52 was progressively improved and upgraded, and the type remained in production until 1964. Since then, its unique blend of performance and payload has made the big bomber difficult to replace.

Although the Stratofortress has been built in eight major production versions (each representing a significant improvement over the previous variant), the B-52H in frontline service today still bears a close external resemblance to the first production B-52A model. Indeed, all Stratofortresses shared a common basic configuration, and apart from the short tail used by the B-52G/H, the different variants were hard to tell apart at a glance. It was the excellence of this basic configuration that laid the foundations for the B-52's longevity, providing a winning combination of adaptability, flexibility and performance.

The bomber's origins lie in the closing months of World War 2, when the US Army Air Force began drawing up requirements for a new generation of post-war bombers, to replace aircraft like the B-36, which was then still to fly! Great emphasis was placed on true inter-continental range to allow the aircraft to carry out its mission without relying on forward bases outside US territory.

Boeing was given a paid study contract for the XB-52 in April 1946, and drew up a conventional looking bomber powered by four 8900 shp Wright T35 turboprops. The Air Force awarded Boeing a contract for a mock-up and two flying prototypes of this design, with the first prototype to be ready by early 1951. At the same time, the company funded its own studies for a more radical turbojet-powered, and swept-winged aircraft. This was made possible by the development of the Pratt & Whitney J57 engine, eight of which were required by Boeing's new heavy bomber.

The company's 'official' B-52 (then still powered by the T53 turbo-prop) offered no real advantages over the existing B-36, and accordingly, the USAF drew up an informal requirement for a jet strategic bomber around Boeing's unpaid, jet-powered XB-52 study. This document was handed to a Boeing team late on the afternoon of Thursday, 21 October 1948, during a meeting which had been scheduled to discuss progress with the 'official' propeller-driven XB-52. During the gathering, the USAF's XB-52 project officer dropped the bombshell that the Air Force was no longer interested in turboprop propulsion!

The Boeing team withdrew to their room in the Van Cleve Hotel in Dayton, where they had produced a detailed three-view drawing by Saturday. On Sunday they built a small model from Balsa wood obtained from a local hobby store, after which the team had its

detailed proposal typed up by a public stenographer. The proposal, drawings and model were on the desk of the XB-52 project officer at Wright Patterson AFB on Monday morning.

This formed the basis of the B-52 configuration which we know today, although there would be detailed changes, and from January 1949 the XB-52 continued as a jet bomber, with the existing contract for two prototypes amended to reflect this.

The XB-52 first flew on 2 October 1952, beaten into the air by the second aircraft following a pneumatic system failure during ground testing. This, the YB-52, flew on 15 April 1952.

The two-and-a-quarter-hour maiden flight took off from Seattle and culminated in a landing at Larson AFB, near Moses Lake, where Boeing Test Pilot 'Tex' Johnson told waiting newsmen, 'I am convinced that this is not only a good aeroplane, it is a hell of a good aeroplane'. But behind the scenes, once the journalists had rushed off to file their stories, Johnson and his Air Force co-pilot, Lt Col Guy M Townsend, were far less complimentary to the Boeing engineers, insisting that they would need new flying suits. 'If we are going to have to manhandle this son-of-a-bitch around, we're going to have arms bigger than our legs, and so we'll need new flight suits'. In fact, the Boeing company tailors were not required, and relatively minor control rigging changes gave the aircraft acceptable control forces and handling characteristics.

The new jet-engined B-52 was evaluated against a modified B-36 derivative (with jet engines and swept wings) proposed by Convair,

The YB-52 is seen here during an early test flight. As seen in the photograph on page six, the Stratofortress was originally designed with tandem cockpits for the two pilots, like that fitted to the much smaller B-47. The navigator was originally intended to sit behind them roughly in line with the point at which the canopy met the fuselage. The bomb-aimer sat facing forward below the navigator, behind the radar scanner (which was mounted below the pilot's seat), while the gunner was to have sat in front of twin 0.50-cal machine guns in the tail (*Author's collection*)

When an SB-17 Flying Fortress (then still in use with Military Air Transport Service as an 'air rescue aeroplane') visited Seattle, Boeing took the opportunity to set up a PR photograph with the YB-52 prototype. The difference in size between the two bombers is readily apparent (*Author's collection*)

Thirteen B-52As were ordered, but only three were built, the rest being completed as B-52Bs. None of the A-models entered frontline service. The first B-52A is seen here with the early style small *UNITED STATES AIR FORCE* legend in full on the nose, along with the bold titling *BOEING B-52A STRATOFORTRESS* (*Author's collection*)

designated the C-60. The latter was the largest jet aircraft in the world (until the C-5A Galaxy flew some 16 years later) and promised huge savings in training, running, support and manufacturing costs. These savings were calculated at an initial $600 million, and at $200 million per year thereafter. Moreover, although the B-60 was 100 mph slower than the B-52, it could carry a much heavier load, and promised to be structurally stronger, with a longer life and greater tolerance to damage or fatigue. But the Boeing's performance edge was vital, and the aircraft was ordered into production.

The same B-52A (52-0001) seen above flies over Washington State during a Boeing test flight. The now familiar side-by-side cockpit layout of the production B-52 was adopted after SAC boss Gen Curtis LeMay had examined the British Vickers Valiant (arguably the most advanced jet bomber then flying), whose cockpit offered better scope for crew co-operation and co-ordination, and which gave more room for enhanced flight instrumentation than did the original tandem cockpit of the XB/YB-52 (*Author's collection*)

The third and final B-52A was later permanently modified for test duties as an NB-52A. As such, the bomber was used as a launch platform for a number of aircraft, including the X-15 (seen here) and NASA's pioneering 'Lifting Bodies'. The aircraft, liberally bedecked with high conspicuity dayglo trim, was nicknamed *The High and Mighty One* (*Author's collection*)

As the Korean War started, Boeing still had a commitment for only the two (XB-52 and YB-52) prototypes, though the USAF had issued a letter of intent for 500 production aircraft. Strategic Air Command (SAC) boss Gen Curtis LeMay argued that his strategic bombing force needed urgent modernisation, and with the outbreak of war in Korea his pleas were listened to more seriously, and the decision to commit the B-52 to production was finally taken early in 1951. The USAF ordered an initial batch of 13 B-52As, with side-by-side seating for the two pilots and a four-foot fuselage stretch. Further orders, for a succession of improved versions, then began to flow thick and fast.

Ten of the B-52As were actually built as convertible RB-52B reconnaissance bombers, along with 17 newly ordered aircraft with provision for a variety of reconnaissance packs in the bomb-bay – 23 more were built as pure B-52B bombers.

Further improvements resulted in the B-52C, 35 of which were constructed with an improved navigation/bombing system, a new alternator and a new fire control system for the tail turret, and with provision for much bigger, 3000-gallon underwing fuel tanks.

As originally built, the B-52D was virtually identical to the last B-52Cs, powered by the same J57-P-19W or -29W engines, and with the same MD-9 fire control system for the tail turret. The only major difference was that the D-model was constructed without the ability to

This B-52B-35-BO (53-0398) was one of three 93rd BW B-52Bs which took part in Operation *Power Flite* – a non-stop, aerial refuelled round the world flight in January 1957. It was flown by Col Chuck Fink, while the lead aircraft (53-0394 *Lucky Lady III*) was piloted by Lt Col James Morris. The undertail position of the brake parachute bay on tall tail B-52s is shown to advantage in this photograph (*Author's collection*)

This B-52C, flaps lowered to allow it to keep station with the accompanying B-17, was never assigned to SAC, serving in the test role as a JB-52C instead. With its tail guns removed, this Stratofortress also lacks the large underwing fuel tanks normally associated with the C-model production variant. After the type's retirement from the frontline, the B-52Cs were redistributed among B-52D units for use as crew trainers – a role which they fulfilled until 1971 (*Philip Jarrett*)

The first Wichita-built B-52D Stratofortress (and also the first D-model to fly, 55-0049) is seen here before delivery to SAC. It lacks the normal 'Milky Way' SAC band and unit markings, which were added later. The D-model was built in large numbers, and would later form the backbone of the bomber effort in the Vietnam War
(*Author's collection*)

The first Wichita-built B-52E (56-0631) is seen here getting smartly airborne on its maiden flight. The E-model's advanced avionics nearly proved to be its undoing, requiring a costly upgrade to solve major reliability issues. The B-52E was never used for conventional bombing, and was therefore not deployed to Vietnam
(*Author's collection*)

carry reconnaissance capsules in its bomb-bay. Boeing built 101 B-52Ds in Seattle, and 69 more rolled out of the company's Wichita plant. In service from 1959, the B-52Ds were modified for the low-level role, with improved navigation and bombing systems, and with the addition of a terrain clearance radar, Doppler and low altitude radar altimeters. The aircraft also underwent an extensive and expensive three-phase structural modification programme.

Before the Vietnam War broke out, few could have predicted the importance which the D-model would assume. Despite being built in large numbers, it had been superseded on the production line by the superior B-52E and F, which formed the tip of SAC's spear. But Vietnam changed all that, and the B-52D, with enhanced ECM and a 'Big Belly' modification which boosted its internal bombload, flew the lion's share of bomber operations in Southeast Asia.

The B-52E was externally identical to the B-52D, but was built from the start for low-level missions, introducing a number of new systems. These included the supposedly more accurate and more reliable (but highly automated) AN/ASQ-38 navigation and AN/ASB-4 bomb

navigation systems. In practice, AN/ASQ-38 proved unreliable, inaccurate and difficult to maintain, and required a major modification programme in order to sort it out – the AN/ASQ-38 system fitted in the F, G and H-models was also upgraded. Some 42 B-52Es were built in Seattle and 58 in Wichita.

Unlike the B-52D which preceded it, and the B-52F which came afterwards, the E-model was never employed as a conventional bombing platform in Vietnam, remaining in the strategic role throughout its entire career.

The B-52F was the last of the 'tall-tailed' B-52 variants, and differed from the B-52E in being powered by eight J57-P-43W, J57-P-43WA, or J57-P-43WB engines, each rated at 13,750 lb st with water injection.

This B-52G-75-BW (57-6471) was the fourth example of the breed, and is seen here during 1959 refuelling trials, still fitted with its original engines. The short tail and small external fuel tanks associated with the B-52G are clearly visible (*Author's collection*)

The B-52G-75-BW seen above was later re-engined with Pratt & Whitney TF33 turbofans, thereby turning it into a de facto prototype for the B-52H, as shown here. The TF33 had very fast throttle response compared to the J57, which was useful in the event of a missed approach or go-around, but flight trials revealed some problems. If the eight throttles were hastily slammed forward, the aircraft would pitch up more quickly than the pilot could correct using the B-52's modest elevator authority, with the rapid increase in power being aggravated by a rapid rearward movement of the fuel in the wing tanks, moving the bomber's centre of gravity further aft. The aircraft later reverted to standard B-52G configuration, and was subsequently modified as a cruise missile carrier, serving with the 2nd BW, before finally being retired on 29 July 1992 (*Author's collection*)

This B-52H-165-BW (61-0010) was one of the aircraft used for trials of the Douglas GAM-87 Skybolt air-launched ballistic missile, and is seen here carrying the full load of four of these weapons. Initial deployment of the Skybolt had originally been scheduled for 1964, but President Kennedy cancelled the programme in December 1962 for political and economic reasons. Interestingly, many years later this particular H-model was modified to carry the AGM-142 'Have Nap' missile, and it remains in frontline service today (*Bruce Robertson*)

The B-52F's paired engines were fitted with 'hard-drive' alternators to supply electrical power to the aircraft, instead of the fuselage-mounted, air-driven turbines and alternators used by earlier versions, which had sometimes caused catastrophic fires, thanks to their proximity to the main fuselage fuel tanks. Seattle built 44 B-52Fs and Wichita built 45 more. The B-52F, with its multiple alternators and excellent performance, was the obvious choice for deployed operations (especially in the tropics), and the modification of 28 B-52Fs under Project 'South Bay', which added a further 24 750-lb bombs on two external pylons, merely increased its usefulness. The B-52F's conventional capabilities led to its early use in Vietnam, and an additional 44 F-models were converted to the same standards.

Originally intended as a redesigned 'Super Buff', the B-52G as built was a more modest improvement of the existing Stratofortress, retaining the J57-P-43WA turbojets used by the B-52F, but with increased water capacity for better take-off performance, and with a revised structure which shaved 15,000 lbs off the empty weight in comparison with the F-model. The wing was built from lighter materials and was extensively redesigned, with the deletion of the aileron system (leaving only the spoilers for roll control) and integral tanks replacing the original rubber 'bladders'. The vertical tailfin was reduced in height by some 91 inches and the tailgunner was relocated to the main cockpit, allowing the weighty pressurised tail cabin of earlier versions to be deleted altogether.

The G-model proved fatiguing to fly, and difficult to fly accurately, being prone to Dutch roll. Its lighter structure and higher fuel capacity soon gave rise to serious structural problems as well, and these required extensive and costly modifications to fix. A total of 193 B-52Gs were built at Wichita.

The final B-52 production variant was the B-52H, which will be described in more detail in a subsequent volume in the *Osprey Combat Aircraft* series.

ATOM-BOMBER – FROM COLD WAR TO CUBA

The B-52 was designed to form the backbone of Strategic Air Command's nuclear deterrent, and performed vital Cold War service by standing ready to fly nuclear strike missions against the USSR, taking over responsibility for the long range strategic role from the mighty Convair B-36.

It had originally been planned that SAC would form seven B-52 wings, equipped with a total of 282 aircraft, although this figure was quickly raised to eleven wings and 495 aircraft (with 45 B-52s per wing, in three squadrons). The first B-52 bombardment wings to form followed this three-squadron structure, but from the late 1950s the threat of intercontinental ballistic missile (ICBM) attack, and the need for dispersal, led to the formation of new strategic wings with single B-52 units, and most of the early three-squadron wings down-sized.

With the increasing possibility that the SAC B-52 force could be destroyed on the ground in a surprise missile attack, the USAF implemented an alert strategy for the wings. Thus, from October 1957, a third of the force, including supporting Boeing KC-135 tankers, was supposed to be permanently available to 'scramble' for a live nuclear attack mission within 15 minutes of the word being given. SAC stated that it had achieved this alert level by May 1960, and in October 1961 claimed to have met the raised alert level (of one half of the force ready to go at the same notice) set by President John F Kennedy in March 1961.

In fact, the actual number of aircraft actually available fell far short of the stated goals, although dozens of B-52s were maintained at immediate readiness on dedicated 'Christmas Tree' flightlines, their crews waiting in adjacent purpose-built alert facilities.

The maintenance of fully-armed B-52s on alert presented a major security headache, necessitating a

The adoption of nuclear alert duties by SAC in October 1957 necessitated beefed up security at its bomber bases. Here, an MP and his dog patrol the 93rd BW's flightline at Castle AFB, California, with the massive bulk of a B-52B looming over both of them (*Author's collection*)

SAC and the RAF's elite V-Force were allies in the deadly business of nuclear deterrence. This photograph of a B-52H and a Vulcan B 2 flying in close formation graphically demonstrates the difference in size between the two aircraft. The Vulcan's huge delta wing gave it superb high altitude performance, but by the 1960s the dawn of the surface-to-air missile had rendered this capability virtually irrelevant (*BAE Systems* via *Author's collection*)

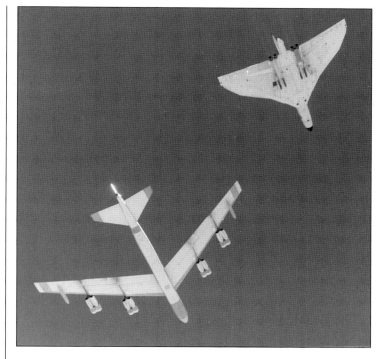

The B-52 was designed to deliver freefall nuclear weapons, and aircraft typically carried a mixture of four of these and some Quail decoys in their capacious bomb-bays. Anti-flash white undersides were added to the B-52 from 1956 to reflect the heat and energy of an atomic blast. The topsides were mainly painted in anti-erosion silver. This aircraft is a B-52B from Castle AFB, taxiing out past a row of KC-97 tankers (*Author's collection*)

heavy and heavily armed security presence on every flightline, rather than just at airfield bomb dumps and weapons stores.

The standard nuclear weapon for the B-52 during the alert era was the B28 series fusion (hydrogen) bomb, introduced in the late 1950s and available in a range of versions, with various yields up to about one megaton. Each B-52 could carry two four-bomb clips in its bomb-bay, although only one clip would usually be loaded, with the remaining space taken up by Quail decoys. The B-52 could also carry the more powerful B41 and B53 fusion bombs, or the 'tactical' B57, which had a yield in the order of about ten kilotons.

From 1959, SAC also introduced the GAM-77 Hound Dog, a rock-et-powered stand-off missile with a one megaton W28 warhead and a 200 (low-level) to 700 nautical mile range. This weapon equipped 29 units, and some 600 had been deployed by late 1963 – these were mainly carried by the B-52E, B-52F, B-52G and B-52H. Hound Dog-equipped aircraft would have used the missiles against enemy defences, helping their penetration in order to deliver the nuclear weapons in their bomb-bays, rather than using them against primary targets.

In the ICBM era, with the likelihood of a 'four-minute warning', a fifteen-minute alert was not a credible deterrent, and emphasis shifted away from static systems which could not launch in under this time. Mobile ICBMs were studied, and increasing importance was attached to the submarine-launched missile force, which could not be so easily destroyed in a pre-emptive strike. For SAC, it became clear that it would have to be able to launch its aircraft within the warning time that would be available if it was to retain any relevance.

This Second Air Force B-52G was, according to the photograph's original caption, pictured during a 'live' airborne alert sortie, although the aircraft (which lacks a SAC band on the nose) is now understood to have been an Edwards-based test machine. The white top to the cockpit and rear fuselage were later additions to the basic SAC strategic colour scheme, helping to protect and cool two vital areas (*Author's collection*)

A Hound Dog missile seen under the first B-52E. The Douglas GAM-77 (later AGM-28) was an early cruise missile, tipped by a one megaton W28 nuclear warhead. The weapon was powered by a 7500 lb st J52 turbojet engine, giving it a stand off range in excess of 600 miles at altitude, and a speed of more than Mach 2. B-52 crews liked the Hound Dog because its engine could be used to provide extra thrust on take off. The missile's fuel tanks could be topped off from those of the B-52, which could in turn be refuelled in flight (*Author's collection*)

In 1963-64, an upgrade programme added pyrotechnic car-
tridge starters to a number of
Stratofortresses. These allowed
all eight engines to be started
simultaneously, thus dramatically
reducing the time it took to get
airborne. This innovation was
accompanied by new procedures,
such as the 'Minimum-Interval
Take-Off' (MITO), which saw
aircraft getting airborne in the
minimum possible time in clouds
of thick black smoke!

Despite these improvements,
SAC realised that crews had to be
kept at cockpit readiness in order
to guarantee that aircraft would be

airborne, and thus far enough away from the blast, before their bases
were hit by enemy missiles. In the spring of 1959 SAC had therefore
proposed that a portion of its force should be maintained on 'airborne
alert', armed and ready to go from an airborne holding pattern. This
was seen as an extension of the ground alert system, ensuring that a
proportion of the overall alert force would be invulnerable to enemy
pre-emptive strikes. It required an astonishing commitment of man-
power, aircraft and resources, and probably only the USA could have
achieved such a feat.

SAC proposal called for a significant proportion of its B-52 force to
be kept on airborne alert, although the expense and complexity of the
scheme meant that only a handful of aircraft were actually assigned to
the commitment.

The bomber wings were brought to higher states of readiness
whenever crisis threatened the USA, most notably when Kennedy and
Khruschev went eyeball-to-eyeball over Cuba in October 1962. The
airborne alert force was considerably strengthened during the Cuban

Missile Crisis, with more aircraft
maintained on 'airborne alert', and
with some of those aircraft moving
forward to orbit just outside Soviet
airspace, waiting for their coded
attack orders.

By mid-1962 there were 22 of
the new strategic wings, each with
a single squadron, while other
wings (some operating in the
training role) controlled a further
11 squadrons. During the Cuban
crisis, some 70 sorties a day maintained the airborne alert at a high
level for about a month, while
those units which were not on

This B-52H scramble was
supposedly 'snapped' during the
Cuban Missile Crisis in 1962. The
crew pictured were from the
4042nd SW at K I Sawyer AFB,
Michigan (*Author's collection*)

Contrails stream from the engines
of a high-flying, Hound Dog armed
B-52. The GAM-77 was initially
carried by all versions of the
Stratofortress apart form the B-52D,
although the latter aircraft received
the weapon late in its career
(*Author's collection*)

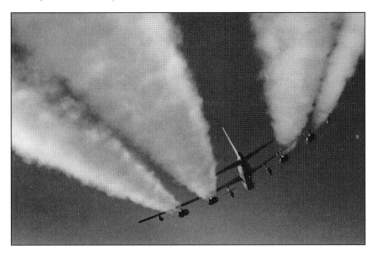

'airborne alert' went to a higher alert posture on the ground, waiting for an order to go which, thankfully, never came. There was a further reorganisation of the B-52 force in 1963 following the Cuban Missile Crisis, SAC's Stratofortress strength being increased to 38 bomb wings – many of the new units resurrected the numberplates of disbanded historic units. Seven of them were designated as Strategic Aerospace Wings, indicating their 'ownership' of an ICBM unit.

After the Cuban Missile Crisis, the airborne alert force was reduced to a more modest (and affordable) level, with 12 nuclear-armed B-52s being kept in the air at any one time. This so-called 'Dirty Dozen' remained on patrol throughout most of the 1960s, before a series of accidents led to the abandonment of the scheme.

A B-52F on airborne alert collided with its KC-135 tanker over Kentucky on 15 October 1959 and crashed with two nuclear weapons on board, although there was no release of radiation. However,

This GAM-77 Hound Dog-armed B-52G-95-BW (58-0159) left behind a typically dense black smoke trail as it took off in front of the base photographer. In an operational Minimum Interval Take Off, the last aircraft in a formation might be taking off in what amounted to full Instrument Meteorological Conditions (IMC). This G-Model was another long-serving 'Buff', ending its career with the 379th BW. Reverting to the conventional bombing role, the aircraft served in Operation *Desert Storm*, flying from Jeddah, in Saudi Arabia, as *Alley Oop's Bold Assault* (*Author's collection*)

The new integral fuel tanks of the B-52G increased internal fuel capacity by 8719 US gallons, allowing the huge 3000-US-gal underwing tanks of previous models to be replaced by much smaller, lighter 700-US-gal tanks, as seen on this Hound Dog-toting B-52G. Even with this reduction, the B-52G still carried 330 US gallons more than the B-52F (*Author's collection*)

Bombing competitions provided an invaluable forum for SAC B-52 crews to practice their skills, with the competitive edge spurring them on to be the 'best they could be'. This 19th BW B-52H was seen at RAF Marham, in Norfolk, in 1967 whilst participating in the *Giant Strike* competition with RAF Bomber Command. It is not known whether the legend on the forward fuselage was intended as an encouragement or an admonition. It reads, *Dear Rocky, not to win is a very Bad Thing*. This B-52H remains in frontline service, and has enjoyed an eventful career. Between 1-3 August 1994, while in the hands of the 2nd BW, the aircraft made a round the world flight as *Lucky Lady IV*, echoing the B-52B flight of January 1957. The aircraft has also served as the Eighth Air Force flagship, and at one time carried the name *Master Blaster* (*Philip Jarrett*)

when a B-52G collided with a KC-135 over Palomeres, in Spain, on 17 January 1966, two of the four bombs on board the bomber were ruptured. This generated great protest in Europe, and required an expensive environmental clean-up. Even more embarrassingly, one the bombs fell into the ocean, requiring an intensive search which took until 15 March.

In late January 1968, the airborne alert system hit the headlines once again when a nuclear-armed B-52G crashed on the Greenland ice pack while trying to perform an emergency landing at Thule AFB, causing another release of radioactive material.

The latter accident signalled the end for the airborne alert system, which had become untenable from military, political and economic standpoints. Meanwhile, SAC's bomber wings continued to stand alert duties, although the loss of aircrew to fight in Southeast Asia on six-month tours of duty placed an increasing strain on their ability to maintain even this commitment. Fortunately, by this time, the US strategic ICBM and SLBM (submarine-launched ballistic missile) force was available to 'take up the slack'.

Bombing competitions also provided an unusual opportunity for extra decoration. This B-52H of the 449th BW (again pictured at RAF Marham) wore a bold '2' on its tailfin, indicating the bomber's assignment to the Second Air Force team. It also had star-spangled intake lips and fuel tanks (*Philip Jarrett*)

SOUTH BAY AND SUN BATH

Although primarily assigned to the nuclear strike mission within SAC, the B-52 was also capable of conducting conventional bombing missions using high-explosive ordnance, and all versions could theoretically carry some 27 500-lb or 750-lb bombs internally, for use in the conventional role. This was a relatively little-practiced capability, since at the height of the Cold War, SAC took its 'Peace is Our Profession' motto and nuclear deterrent role very seriously, and regarded everything else as being an unwelcome diversion of attention from what was the 'primary responsibility'.

But while SAC might not have wanted any of its B-52s diverted to conventional bombing duties, the USAF saw the aircraft as offering considerable potential in the role, and was determined that at least a portion of the B-52 fleet would have a real conventional capability.

By the early 1960s the B-52B and C were nearing the end of their service careers, and were already assigned to the nuclear strike and reconnaissance roles, while the B-52D had been modified for low-level nuclear strike duties. The B-52E had been specifically designed for low-level operations, and had only been built in small numbers. The B-52F was similarly equipped, but offered a number of advantages which made it the best suited variant for conventional bombing duties.

Although the F-model was the last of the 'tall-tailed' B-52 variants, it was in many respects the first 'second generation' 'Buff', with its water-injected 13,750 lb st J57-P-43W, -43WA or -43WB engines, and with engine-driven 'hard-drive' alternators (rather than fuselage-mounted, air-driven turbines and alternators) supplying electrical power to the aircraft.

With its multiple alternators and excellent performance, the B-52F was the obvious choice for deployed operations, and the type was also fitted with hardpoints and wiring provision to carry GAM-77 (later AGM-28) Hound Dog missiles underwing. It was always clear that these pylons could easily be converted to carry suspension beams and ejector racks for conventional bombs. The B-52F was, therefore,

Boeing's original caption for this photograph read, 'B-52 Global Bomber displays non-nuclear capability'. This aircraft (Wichita-built 2nd BW B-52F-70-BW 57-0162) undertook conventional bombing trials in 1964, carrying a variety of loads on its modified 'Hound Dog' pylons. Here, the aircraft carries six 750-lb bombs under each wing on short multiple ejector rack (MER) beams, with outer attachment points unused. The aircraft is thoroughly representative of the first *South Bay*-modified F-models deployed to Guam. After a long and productive life, 57-0162 was assigned to MASDC on 15 September 1971 (*Author's collection*)

the variant chosen to receive an enhanced conventional bombing capability in 1964, even before the need to deploy B-52s to Vietnam had become apparent.

The Seattle-built 93rd BW B-52F 57-0034 undertook armament tests at Eglin, carrying 12 500-lb bombs under each wing, while the Wichita-built 2nd BW B-52F 57-0162 undertook trials in Boeing's hands, carrying a variety of loads on its modified Hound Dog pylons. The modification was straightforward, and was quickly proven.

A total of 28 B-52Fs were initially modified to the same standards under Project *South Bay*, with their Hound Dog pylons adapted to carry multiple ejector racks, with four triple ejectors in 'line astern'. These allowed the B-52F to carry 12 standard 500- or 750-lb bombs under each wing, with 27 500-, 750- or 1000-lb bombs in the bomb-bay, increasing the total bombload to 51 750-lb bombs. The primary

By the time this B-52F-105-BO (57-0039) of the 93rd BW was seen at RAF Marham in 1967, participating in the first USAF/RAF Bombing and Navigation Competition, it was a combat veteran, having flown *Arc Light* missions over Vietnam. The competition was known as *Giant Strike* to the USAF and *Double Top* to Bomber Command. The aircraft was retired to the 'boneyard' on 19 July 1971 (*Philip Jarrett*)

The tail of 57-0039, showing the manned, four-gun turret fitted to most tall-tailed B-52s, with its distinctive 'horned' ECM antennas on each side of the gun-laying radar. Some B-52Bs had a twin M-24A-1 20 mm cannon installation, with an A-3A fire control system, but most early 'Buffs' had this quad 0.50-cal turret. The G-model retained these guns, but moved the gunner forward onto the flightdeck, where he enjoyed greater comfort, but to see behind the aircraft he relied on radar (and a primitive video camera whose resolution was 'good enough to tell night from day, or to see whether the brake 'chute had deployed') (*Bruce Robertson*)

weapons used by the B-52F operationally, however, were the M117 750-lb HE bomb and the BLU-3 Cluster Bomb Unit (CBU).

Following attacks by Viet Cong (VC) guerrillas on US forces in South Vietnam in early 1965, the US retaliated with a series of limited (*Flaming Dart*) strikes on North Vietnamese targets. In January 1965 some 32 KC-135 tankers were deployed to Kadena AFB, on Okinawa, to form the new 4252nd SW. Although intended initially to support Pacific Air Forces fighter-bombers operating in Vietnam, the KC-135 force was also large enough to support the deployment of B-52s.

In February 1965 some 30 B-52Fs (principally the *South Bay* aircraft) from the 2nd BW at Barksdale and the 320th BW at Mather were transferred to Anderson AFB, on the island of Guam, coming under the control of the 3960th SW. Guam (often known simply as 'the Rock') was a small (32-mile-long) island which rose 32,000 ft out of the Marianas Trench, and which housed Andersen AFB and a smaller emergency airstrip. Crews for the deployed B-52Fs were initially drawn from the 2nd BW's 20th BS (replaced by the 7th BW's 9th BS from Carswell in early May) and from the 320th BW's 441st BS.

This marked a relatively subtle shift in USAF power in the region, since the B-52Fs replaced a smaller force of B-52Bs at Andersen which had been maintaining a nuclear 'reflex alert' at the base. Moreover, although the theatre commander in South Vietnam, US Army Gen William Westmoreland, wanted to use the B-52Fs immediately to carpet-bomb VC enclaves in South Vietnam, such a step was viewed as being extremely controversial, and the bombers were held in reserve for several months.

The US State Department feared that using the B-52Fs would represent a major escalation of the conflict, confirming the dire predictions from those who opposed the US involvement that the war was spiralling out of control. There

Unusually, this B-52F-70-BW (57-0164) is seen carrying only four 750-lb M117 bombs on its underwing pylons. The photograph was dated May 1965, perhaps indicating that this was a training sortie, if accurate. Although only 11 spaces separated 57-0153 (in the photograph directly opposite) and 57-0164 on the Wichita production line, one has a black upper radome, while the others is white (*Robert F Dorr*)

The fact that this anonymous B-52F (its old-style nose radome and escape hatches, combined with under-engine scoops, give away that this is an F-model) is refuelling with its gear down suggests that the tanker passing fuel is a piston-engined KC-97 (*Author's collection*)

Having demonstrated the F-model's conventional bombing capabilities at Eglin AFB during 1964, the 2nd BW participated in the first *Arc Light* attack against VC targets in South Vietnam on 18 June 1965. Here, the wing's 57-0153 (a B-52F-65-BW) is seen taking off on that first strike, carrying 12 M117 750-lb bombs under each wing (*Robert F Dorr*)

The huge distance between Guam and Vietnam meant that inflight refuelling was always required on operations until the introduction of the longer range B-52G. Here, B-52E-85-BO 56-0635 is seen taking gas from an early, short-tailed KC-135A tanker during a stateside training mission (*Author's collection*)

was also the very real worry that any losses would be seen as a major international humiliation, while actually selecting targets against which the B-52 would be useful, without being entirely disproportionate, was also a problem. Nor was SAC enthusiastic about seeing its B-52s used in the tactical role, and diverting B-52Fs to support a 'brushfire war' in the Far East was regarded by many senior officers as an unwelcome, troublesome and irritating diversion from the primary SAC mission.

From Westmoreland's perspective, the B-52 promised to be a useful tool – operating as an airborne heavy artillery barrage which would be able to bring enormous firepower to bear on his elusive enemy. The VC could be attacked even in their jungle sanctuaries, destroying base camps and tunnel networks without having to commit vulnerable ground troops. The B-52s could even operate above the weather in conditions which would have grounded the fighter-bombers, whose weapon loads were, in any case, too small to be of any significance against many target sets.

In order to allow the B-52s to operate effectively, the USAF deployed an MSQ-77 *Combat Skyspot/Combat Proof* radar beacon to Tan Son Nhut. This could be used by the B-52 crew as a highly accurate navigation beacon, with an operator who could pass corrections and bomb release indications at ranges of up to 100 miles. *Skyspot* could be used to guide B-52s to new, unbriefed targets of opportunity, and allowed B-52s to attack targets which did not have a distinctive radar signature. By June 1967, seven *Skyspots* were operational, bringing most of the war zone within reach.

It was clear, therefore, that it would only be a matter of time before the B-52Fs were committed, and in anticipation of this, a further 46 F-models were modified to the enhanced conventional bombing standard under *Sun Bath*. This brought the total number of available B-52F conventional bombers to 72 aircraft, although fewer than half were deployed to Guam at any one time.

The first *Arc Light* mission (the first B-52 combat mission in Southeast Asia) was finally launched on 18 June 1965, when 30 B-52Fs left Anderson to perform a tactical strike on VC forces at Ben Cat – a widely dispersed base area 40 miles north of Saigon. The B-52Fs operated in ten three-ship cells, each with a phonetically distinct colour call sign. Midway to the target, near the Philippines, the first cell of three B-52s (Green Cell) prepared to rendezvous with the KC-135s from Kadena, each planning to take on 89,000 lbs of fuel in a 17-minute contact. Things then began to go badly awry.

The first cell arrived early and began to circle to use up time, but turned back across the path of Blue Cell and into the path of Yellow Cell. Two aircraft (57-0047 and 57-0179) collided, destroying both bombers and killing eight of the twelve crew. Another B-52F was forced to abort the mission and divert to Kadena with technical failures (losing a hydraulic pump and its radar), and the remaining 27 aircraft

The difference in size between the 'Buff' and the Stratotanker is clearly evident in this view of JB-52C-50-BO 54-2676 and KC-135A 55-3118. The USAF's 'boom' method of inflight refuelling was easier for the bomber pilot, and allowed the transfer of fuel at much higher rates than could be achieved using the 'probe and drogue' method, which was more suitable for refuelling smaller tactical aircraft (*Author's collection*)

This B-52F-65-BW (57-0144) was named the *Mekong Express*, and is seen here just releasing a stick of 750-lb bombs, six of which are visible, with up to 45 more to follow. A bomb tally is worn on the nose (below the 'IR F' in US Air Force), and the aircraft has black undersides. The *Mekong Express* was retired to the 'boneyard' in November 1967 (*Philip Jarrett*)

Another view of the *Mekong Express*, seen here during its 22nd mission in October 1965, crossing the coast en route back to Guam. The aircraft went on to complete 86 missions. B-52 pilots of the period generally regarded the F-Model as the best 'Buff', and many were disappointed when the variant was retired, instead of receiving Phase V ECM equipment (*Robert F Dorr*)

achieved little because the enemy had largely left the area by the time the survivors dropped their bombs, only half of which actually landed in the target area. The mission, costing $20 million, killed two enemy soldiers and destroyed 40 'barracks' buildings, a communications centre and a rice store.

SAC immediately revised its refuelling procedures, separating refuelling corridors by altitude and adding a complex series of timing triangles which aircraft could use in order to safely reach their tankers on time. The revised system worked well, and no further B-52s came close to collision during seven years of *Arc Light* operations.

A planned second June *Arc Light* mission was cancelled when it was learned that the enemy had again fled the intended target area, and it was not until July that the B-52Fs returned to combat, flying five more *Arc Light* raids, totalling 140 sorties. A further five raids (totalling 165 sorties) were flown during August.

Each B-52 raid still had to be individually approved by the White House, and by the time a request from MACV had been passed to SAC, approved by CINCPAC, approved by the Joint Chiefs of Staff, approved by the President and then passed back down the chain to Anderson for execution, considerable time had elapsed. The B-52 was not a weapon which could be used 'reactively', nor against a mobile or changing target.

By late August, decision-making authority for *Arc Light* missions had been moved down slightly from the White House to the Joint Chiefs of Staff, although the approval chain was still time consuming and unwieldy, and the obvious solution (of passing control to Gen Momyer's Seventh Air Force) was resisted.

By August, the B-52Fs at Andersen were being flown by crews from the Carswell-based 7th BW's 9th and 20th BSs, who saw a steady build up in missions, albeit that these were often flown by smaller formations of aircraft – and even by single cells of three B-52Fs, attacking multiple locations simultaneously. Some 322 sorties were flown during September, before the monthly sortie rate settled closer to 300.

The USAF also revised its tactics, and, from November, the B-52Fs began to fly missions in direct support of ground troops. After five days of bombing attacks against a secret North Vietnamese Army

(NVA) base (housing two regiments) near the USMC Fire Base at Plei Me, in the Central Highlands, in which 1795 tons of bombs were dropped in 98 sorties, the marine base itself came under attack. B-52Fs were called in to prevent a massive enemy assault from the Ia Drang valley, with 18 aircraft dropping 344 tons of bombs.

This was virtually the last major mission for the 7th BW's crews, who 'shipped home' in December, making way for the final deployment by B-52F units. The last squadrons deployed were the 320th BW's 441st BS (making its second visit) and the 454th BW's 736th BS from Colombus AFB, Ohio.

During Operation *Harvest Moon*, on 12 December 1965, USMC troops mopping up near Da Nang came under attack, and Gen Lewis W Walt requested close air support. He watched in astonishment from his helicopter as B-52s smashed the enemy force, also uncovering a network of caves, tunnels and bunkers in which the USMC found 60 enemy dead. A grateful Walt cabled SAC's C-in-C, Gen John D Ryan, informing him that;

'We are more than impressed with the results. We are delighted. The timing was precise, the bombing accurate and the overall effects awesome to behold. The enemy has abandoned his prepared positions and much of his equipment in great confusion, and this is making our part of the job easier.'

That same day the B-52Fs also expanded their area of operations into neighbouring Laos, supporting the ongoing *Steel Tiger/Cricket/Tiger Hound* counter-insurgency operations aimed at removing the sanctuary offered to NVA and VC forces in this neutral country.

Some 24 B-52Fs, laden with M117 HE bombs and BLU-3 CBUs, participated in the first Laotian *Arc Light*, which was not notified to the Laotian Prime Minister Souvanna Phouma. Thereafter, there were two categories of Laotian *Arc Light*, consisting of Category 1 targets, which were to be notified to the Laotians, and Category 2 targets, which were not.

The B-52Fs flew two more Laotian *Arc Light*s in February 1966, Operation *West Stream* with 12 aircraft and Operation *Back Road* with 27 bombers. The latter attacked a target in Kontum Province on 27 February, and was followed up by the insertion of a *Shining Brass* damage evaluation team. It found that three quarters of the M117s had missed the target area altogether, and most of the rest had exploded harmlessly in the jungle canopy. Five more raids were undertaken in Laos in March. These raids were authorised by the US ambassador to Laos, William H Sullivan, who became so fond of the B-52 that he later acquired the nickname 'Arc Light Sullivan'.

In the event, none of the missions were notified until September 1966. Whether notified or not, the Laotian B-52 raids were covert, and the majority were 'covered' by diversionary raids by smaller numbers of B-52s on the Vietnamese side of the border, in the same general area. Had attention been drawn to the attacks in Laos, these could have been dismissed as a 'mis-reporting' of the target area, or as navigational errors by aircraft attacking Vietnamese targets. The war in Laos thus remained a shadowy affair at the time, and is still largely unknown to this day.

When the Laotian Government was finally informed about these raids, it imposed conditions on them, although most of these were already being observed. *Arc Lights* over Laos were to be flown only at night, and at altitudes in excess of 30,000 ft, sticking to a 60-mile wide corridor which avoided major population centres.

The B-52Fs did not range into North Vietnam, which remained the exclusive territory of the USAF's tactical fighters, principally the Republic F-105 Thunderchief. Thus the USAF used its tactical aircraft in a strategic role, and strategic aircraft in a tactical role!

Even in 1966, the war in Vietnam was contentious, and not something for a career-minded Hollywood actor to be seen to be supporting too strongly. The B-52F deployment was therefore doubly pleased when a USAF Reserve brigadier general arrived at Andersen AFB as part of a two-week inspection tour, since that officer was none other than Jimmy Stewart. Coming to the end of his USAF service, he had reached the rank of brigadier general in the USAF Reserve in 1959.

During his two weeks of active duty in 1966 Stewart requested a combat assignment, and he was duly sent on an inspection tour of Vietnam, where his stepson, 1Lt Ronald McLean, had recently been killed at age 24. Stewart was a keen aviator and a great patriot, and he insisted on participating in a bombing strike against VC targets, flying a mission at the controls of B-52F 57-0149.

Although best known to the general public as a Hollywood actor, Stewart had also enjoyed a remarkable and distinguished military career. He had seen the war clouds gathering and volunteered for service in 1940, joining the USAAC in March 1941 – a full nine months before the Japanese attack on Pearl Harbor and the United States' entry into the war. At the age of 33, Stewart was too old to be an aviation cadet, but used his own aircraft (a Stinson 105) to build hours until he qualified to enter as an experienced pilot. The gangling Stewart was also underweight, according to the Army Air Corps doctors, and he binged until he had put on the ten pounds necessary to meet the Army's minimum weight requirement.

Successively flying BT-13s as an instructor, and later piloting twin-Beeches and Boeing B-17s, Stewart craved overseas combat duty, and made considerable efforts to overcome official reluctance to place him in harm's way, and to avoid the propaganda duties which were being marked out for him.

Assigned to the 445th BG as operations officer, Capt Stewart flew B-24s from Tibenham, in Norfolk, leading the group during a 1000-bomber raid against Berlin on 22 Mach 1944 and rising to command the 703rd BS. Stewart was transferred to the 453rd BG after that unit had suffered heavy losses, and with him as operations officer and a new CO at the helm, the 453rd's proficiency rate on raids rose from near the bottom of the list to near the top among Eighth Air Force units.

Stewart became a full colonel and the 2nd BW's chief of staff in July 1944, and then in the spring of 1945 became the wing CO. He flew 20 bombing missions over Germany (against targets which included Brunswick, Bremen, Frankfurt, Schweinfurt and Berlin), and his decorations included the *Croix de Guerre* (with palm), two Distinguished Flying Crosses, a succession of oak leaf clusters, seven battle stars and an Air Medal. Careful to avoid being known for who he was before the war, rather than what he was doing in uniform, Stewart gained an enviable reputation as an exceptionally hardworking, conscientious and dedicated officer

Even after resuming his acting career, Stewart continued to take his Air Force Reserve duties extremely seriously, and ensured that he flew the B-36, B-47, B-52 and B-58. During the war, he had been a keen student of bomber tactics and doctrine, and had developed a real knowledge of, and enthusiasm for, daylight precision bombing. His exposure to the carpet-bombing of area targets in Vietnam must have come as something of a shock to the distinguished brigadier general.

During their period in Vietnam, the USAF's B-52Fs flew about 300 sorties per month on average. The aircraft retained their standard SAC silver colour scheme, with glossy 'anti-flash' white undersides and full unit markings. The aircraft wore the 'star-spangled' 'Milky Way' SAC ribbon around their noses, with the SAC shield superimposed on the port side and a wing badge to starboard. Some 7th and 93rd BW B-52Fs also wore a narrow red chord-wise band on their tailfins immediately below their serial numbers, and some aircraft gained individual names and small, discrete pieces of nose-art. Many were decorated with bomb-logs and, even though the aircraft were only in-theatre for a relatively short time, several amassed respectable mission tallies, with the very first B-52F, 57-0139 *Lady Luck*, becoming the first aircraft to reach 100 missions.

From about October 1965, many B-52Fs in Southeast Asia had their anti-flash white undersides hastily (and often crudely) repainted black to reduce their conspicuity during night attacks, with the black colour covering the same areas that had hitherto been anti-flash white. A handful of aircraft also received reflective stripes on their underwing fuel tanks to aid conspicuity at night when parked on the ground, but this feature was more associated with the B-52D.

The B-52Fs were replaced by B-52Ds in Vietnam, and all had returned to the USA by the beginning of April 1966, having dropped more than 100,000 tons of bombs on enemy targets. Just prior to the aircraft returning home, there was an organisational change at Andersen which saw a new provisional wing – the 4133rd BW (Provisional) – established to manage the deployed B-52s.

This unarmed B-52F-110-BO (57-0065) was pictured in service with 'Buff' training unit, the 93rd BW. This particular aircraft was finally retired to MASDC on 9 August 1971 (*Author's collection*)

THE *BIG BELLY* B-52D JOINS *ARC LIGHT*

The overall pattern of B-52 activities for most of the Vietnam War had been set during the B-52F's brief period of operations. Thereafter, the 'Buff' operated primarily against tactical and semi-tactical targets in South Vietnam and Laos, occasionally venturing into the southern region of North Vietnam just above the demilitarised zone (DMZ) between South and North Vietnam. The aircraft usually operated in small units – often in three aircraft cells – and bombed by radar, or under the control of *Skyspot*.

Even during the B-52F deployments, the 'Buff' had become one of Gen Westmoreland's 'weapons of choice', providing him with the 'heavy artillery' he felt to be necessary to defeat the enemy at an acceptable cost in American lives by dumping overwhelming firepower on enemy concentrations, even when their precise location could not be ascertained. Westmoreland was also mindful of the B-52's psychological effect, and appreciated the way in which a single cell of three bombers could cut a swathe miles long through the jungle in which nothing could survive unscathed.

Moreover, the aircraft dropped their bombs from such a height that the enemy had no idea they were under attack until the explosions began, with deadly effect from flying shrapnel or simply from the colossal blast effects. Indeed, there were reports of damage assessment teams finding entire enemy units dead without a mark on them, killed by concussion and over-pressure. Survivors of B-52 attacks were at best severely demoralised and at worst completely shell-shocked, and spread fear of the aircraft to troops who had not been 'on the receiving end'.

Gen Westmoreland later remarked that;

'We know, from talking to prisoners and defectors, that the enemy troops fear B-52s, tactical air, artillery and armour in that order.'

The B-52D looked sinister and purposeful in the new camouflage scheme adopted for use over Southeast Asia. The black undersides were less conspicuous (when viewed from the ground) when the aircraft cruised at very high altitude, whereas white aircraft could sometimes 'glint' and betray their position. It was not intended as night camouflage. B-52D-55-BO 55-0087 served until 1982 (*Author's collection*)

The B-52Fs had even demonstrated some success against the jungle tunnel complexes that so frustrated American ground forces, although the subsequent introduction of B-52Ds armed with heavy bombs that had been fitted with delayed-action fuses increased the aircraft's effectiveness against such targets. The newly fused bombs buried themselves deeply into the ground before detonating, sending a shock wave through the ground which caved in the tunnels.

The B-52Fs at Andersen AFB were replaced by B-52Ds from March 1966. Before the Vietnam War, the B-52D had been a specialised low-level nuclear strike aircraft, having been modified for the low-level role from 1959 through the introduction of structural improvements, terrain clearance radar, Doppler, low altitude radar altimeters and uprated navigation and bombing systems.

The B-52Ds had also undergone a four-phase electronic counter-measures (ECM) improvement programme. Phase I had aimed to provide the minimum ECM equipment that was necessary to counter the Soviet radar and SAM threat, while Phase II, retrofitted to earlier B-52 variants between November 1959 and September 1963, introduced the same Quick Reaction Capability package that was installed in new-build B-52Hs. Under Phase III of the programme the B-52D finally received ECM equipment comparable to the cancelled AN/ALQ-27 system that had originally been planned as part of the aircraft's low-level conversion.

By the time it became clear that the Stratofortress commitment in Vietnam would be long term, the B-52B had already been retired and the B-52E force was too small to be significant, having been assigned to the more important strategic nuclear role with Hound Dog cruise missiles, like the later B-52Gs and new B-52Hs. Low-level penetration for strategic nuclear bombers was already seen as being old fashioned and 'behind the times', and this led some to seek a new role for the B-52D, which was in service in large numbers, with many crews trained and available to sustain a deployment in Southeast Asia.

Beginning in late 1965, all surviving B-52Ds were modified to give them an enhanced conventional bombing capability. This included the

The white-painted cockpit identifies this drone-carrying 'Buff' as 60-0036 (a B-52H-150-BW), one of two aircraft converted to launch the D-21B *Tagboard* reconnaissance drone. The aircraft flew operational missions from Andersen AFB, Guam, Kadena AB, Okinawa, and Hickam AFB, Hawaii, sending their drones out over communist China. 60-0036, now named *Tagboard Flyer*, was eventually transferred from the 72nd BS at Minot AFB to Edwards AFB, where it is still in use today (*Author's collection*)

B-52D-55-BO 55-0068 was one of the first D-models to be modified under the *Big Belly* programme, and is seen here at Wichita, pristine in its new camouflage. The aircraft survived its participation in Vietnam, and was eventually preserved at Lackland AFB, Texas (*Author's collection*)

same wing pylon modifications that had been applied to the *South Bay* and *Sun Bath* B-52Fs, combined with the so-called 'high density bombing' (HDB) or *Big Belly* upgrade. Under this, the bomb-bay was modified to allow the internal carriage of up to 84 Mk 82 500-lb or 42 M117 750-lb bombs. There was no increase in the internal dimensions of the bomb-bay, and no use of bulged bomb-bay doors, and the increase was achieved by using new high-density 'clips' of bombs. This gave the *Big Belly* B-52D a total maximum bombload of 60,000 lbs – about 22,000 lbs more than the B-52F had carried.

The *Big Belly* programme also saw the development of a new 'preload system' under which clips of bombs could be pre-prepared for rapid loading, reducing the time required to rearm the big bombers, or to reconfigure an aircraft with different weapons. The *Big Belly* B-52Ds retained their ability to carry up to four freefall nuclear weapons, and could also carry mines. The programme costs totalled $30.6 million overall.

While the B-52Fs deployed to Guam had retained their standard SAC colour scheme, sometimes with their undersides hastily daubed in black, the B-52Ds modified under the HDB upgrade were completely repainted in a new purpose-designed camouflage scheme. This consisted of a set camouflage pattern of dark green (FS 34079), blue green (FS 34159) and tan (FS 24201 or 34201) on the uppersurfaces of the fuselage, wings and tailplanes, which was very much like the camouflage applied to F-100s, F-105s, F-4s and other tactical aircraft. But while these tactical types had pale grey or white undersides, the B-52Ds had black (FS 17038 or 27038) undersides, with black fuselage sides and a black tailfin. National insignia was reduced to a

B-52D-75-BO 56-0603 was another early *Big Belly* aircraft. The way in which the wingtip outriggers remained clear of the ground when the aircraft was lightly loaded is clearly evident in this view. This aircraft was one of those sent to MASDC in the first big batch of D-model retirements between August and December 1978 (*Author's collection*)

tiny size, and serial numbers and other markings were all applied in low-conspicuity dull red.

When newly painted at stateside depots, the camouflaged B-52Ds looked extremely smart. However, in the harsh climate in Southeast Asia the paint weathered quickly, and when scuffed to a dull matt finish crews began to notice a reduction in the bombers' performance. Bomb logs and nose art, which had become common on the B-52Fs, were extremely rare (but not entirely unknown) on the B-52D, and even the SAC band and unit markings were initially omitted.

About 42 B-52s were initially committed to the war, although the number of aircraft deployed gradually rose to double that number. A total of eleven B-52D wings eventually undertook 'en masse' *Arc Light* deployments to Southeast Asia, some of them completing three combat tours. The wings involved were the 22nd BW from March AFB, the 28th BW from Ellsworth, the 91st BW from Glasgow, the 92nd SAW from Fairchild, the 96th SAW from Dyess, the 99th BW from Westover, the 306th BW from McCoy, the 454th BW from Columbus, the 461st BW from Amarillo, the 484th BW from Turner and the 509th BW from Pease.

Other units, normally flying the B-52E, F, G and H, supplied large numbers of air- and groundcrew to support these deployments, but did not themselves transfer to Southeast Asia 'en masse'. A handful of B-52D units did not deploy either, including the 340th BW from Bergstrom.

The first B-52Ds arrived at Andersen in early March 1966, with the 28th BW replacing the B-52Fs of the 320th. Later that same month the 48th BW sent a further deployment of *Big Belly* B-52Ds to relieve the 454th BW's last B-52Fs.

Shortly after the B-52Ds had taken over at Andersen, aircraft were sent north, across the DMZ into Route Pack 1, the southernmost part of North Vietnam. Their purpose was to interdict 'strands' of the Ho Chi Minh Trail (Vietnam's principal supply route for VC guerrillas and regular NVA forces operating in the south) as they went through the Ban Karai, Ban Raving and Mu Gia passes. The first attack (Operation *Rock Kick II*) was made against the Mu Gia pass on 11 April 1966, and reportedly represented the largest single bombing attack since

World War 2, with the delivery of 600 tons of bombs. The $21 million mission involved 30 B-52Ds, each carrying 24 1000-lb bombs internally, with 24 750-lb bombs underwing, and closed Route 15 for about 20 hours. A follow-up raid was undertaken on 26 April, leaving 32 craters in the road, although again these were filled in within a day. The two attacks together totalled 44 sorties. There was then a five-month hiatus in attacks against North Vietnamese targets.

During April and May 1966, the B-52Ds also flew *Arc Lights* in support of Operation *Birmingham* – a major search and destroy operation in Tay Ninh. Fourteen enemy base camps were bombed, and the B-52Ds expended more than 3118 tons of bombs (including 220 tons of CBUs) in 162 sorties. A total of 453 buildings were destroyed, containing 1267 tons of rice.

On 14 September 1966 Capt Charles Elson of the 28th BW, deployed to Andersen from Ellsworth AFB, in South Dakota, took off on what would be the 5000th B-52 sortie of the war. By that point, the Stratofortresses had dropped a staggering 95,000 tons of bombs, despite a bomb shortage which had imposed a 600-sortie limit for most months of 1966.

When attacks against the north resumed, ten missions (150 sorties) were flown against 'Tally Ho' – an area perceived as being a major base complex – between 15-26 September. During one of these missions a 454th BW B-52D, piloted by Thomas C Dorsey, was unexpectedly engaged by two SA-2 SAMs. Fortunately, the crew's alert electronic warfare officer (EWO) picked up the 'Fan Song' guidance radar and the bomber turned smartly out towards the coast in the hope of easing the task of what the crew expected would be an inevitable search and rescue mission. Luckily, the EWO managed to jam the two missiles, which exploded a scant, but safe, 3000 ft from the bomber. It was felt that the loss of a B-52 to a SAM would provide the enemy with an unacceptably powerful propaganda victory, and attacks across the DMZ were quickly called off.

The incident hastened an upgrade of the B-52D's electronic warfare equipment, which was already the most comprehensive fitted to any B-52 model. The *Rivet Rambler* programme resulted in the installation of what was called the Phase V ECM fit, which included one AN/ALR-18 automated set-on receiving set, one AN/ALR-20 panoramic receiver set, one AN/APR-25 radar homing and warning system, four AN/ALT-6B or AN/ALT-22 continuous wave jamming transmitters, two AN/ALT-16 barrage-jamming systems, two AN/ALT-32H and one AN/ALT-32L high- and low-band jamming sets, six AN/ALE-20 flare dispensers (96 flares) and eight AN/ALE-24 chaff dispensers (1125 bundles).

B-52D-60-BO 55-0100 amassed 5000 combat hours during its participation in Vietnam, and was eventually retired to become the permanent *Arc Light* memorial at Andersen AFB. The aircraft is seen here dropping a stick of 500-lb Mk 82 bombs, which became one of the best-known images of the war. Interestingly, the bomber has a replacement tail gun turret, which is still painted in the original anti-flash white (*Robert F Dorr*)

During October 1966, the B-52Ds flew *Arc Lights* against the trail in Quang Tri province under the acronym SLAM (Seek, Locate, Annihilate and Monitor), some 225 sorties being flown to help relieve a Special Forces camp near Suoi Da. Operations during November included *Attleboro*, with 200 *Arc Light* sorties dropping 4000 tons of bombs and destroying many VC buildings and stores, including rice. The operation was also said to have killed a VC general.

During 1967, the B-52Ds flew 396 sorties during SLAM III, SLAM IV, SLAM V and SLAM VI against different parts of the Ho Chi Minh Trail, with varying degrees of success. Between 8-26 January, under Operation *Cedar Falls*, B-52Ds collapsed a huge tunnel complex near Saigon, setting off numerous secondary explosions as VC weapons dumps were destroyed. A further 126 *Arc Light* sorties were flown during February-May 1967 as part of Operation *Junction City*. These missions were the first to be flown in direct support of ground troops, and resulted in a body count of 2700 enemy dead.

Andersen AFB was far from ideal as a location for B-52 operations over Vietnam. Guam lay 2600 miles from Saigon, necessitating very long, 12-14 hour missions during which fatigue was a constant danger, and which almost certainly contributed to a high accident rate. The distances involved also tied up large numbers of tankers, and piled the flying hours onto the already structurally-tired B-52s.

On 7 July 1967 the 3rd Air Division lost its CO, Maj Gen William J Crumm, when his wingman collided with his aircraft as they turned onto their attack heading at the IP. Both aircraft (56-0595 and 56-0627) crashed, killing six crewmen, although seven baled out successfully.

Another aircraft was lost the following day when its pilot misjudged his emergency landing (with no flaps and several engines out) at

B-52D-80-BO 56-0613 taxies out at Andersen AFB. Bombs were often loaded 'the old fashioned way' on Guam, whilst at U-Tapao pre-loaded clips were the norm. White stripes on the underwing fuel tanks were added to try and prevent vehicles colliding with aircraft on the ground at night, and the 'last three' ('613') superimposed on the tank stripe could help a new crew find their assigned aircraft in the sprawling acres of revetments and hardstands (*Robert F Dorr*)

Da Nang, running off the end of the runway and exploding. In both accidents, tiredness was probably a factor.

Andersen's runway was also short for a fully-laden B-52D, with a dip in the middle and an uphill gradient towards the normal take-off end. Even without an engine failure, many aircraft dipped as they went off the end of the runway, which was on the edge of a 500-ft cliff, and it could take up to ten minutes for a B-52 to accelerate to its climb speed of 280 kts. It could prove frightening for the Russian intelligence 'trawler' cruising off the end of the runway.

But it was distance, more than any other factor, which mitigated against the use of Guam. The USAF looked at basing B-52s closer to the scene of the action, in Taiwan, the Philippines, or Okinawa, before settling on Thailand as being the ideal location for a second operating location.

The Royal Thai Navy airfield of Sattahip, more widely known as U-Tapao was already used by SAC KC-135s, and soon became the favoured choice for a second B-52 base. The US Ambassador was first asked to examine the possibility of using U-Tapao in September 1966, although Defence Secretary Robert McNamara then proposed an alternative plan, suggesting that facilities at Andersen be uprated to allow a larger B-52 force, with a second small Forward Operating Location (FOL) for 15 aircraft at Tuy Hoa, in South Vietnam itself. There was near-universal opposition to this idea, and McNamara directed the ambassador to continue his efforts in January 1967.

The Thais approved the request in March 1967, and the first three bombers arrived at U-Tapao Royal Thai Air Base on 10 April to participate in Operation *Poker Dice*. By this time, B-52 numbers at

Its refuelling receptacle doors already open, a B-52D manoeuvres behind its tanker prior to closing up on the extended flying boom. This photo actually dates from April 1982's *Team Spirit* exercise, although only the lack of underwing bombs gives away the fact that this was not a routine wartime *Arc Light* mission (*Robert F Dorr*)

Andersen had grown to 61 aircraft, which was more than the base could really handle. Initially, U-Tapao was used as a forward base only, with all major maintenance work, mission planning and scheduling continuing at Andersen. Some B-52Ds would fly a routine bombing mission from Anderson, but would then land at U-Tapao, from where they would fly eight further return 'round robin' trips, before undertaking a final raid to land back at Anderson.

The distance from U-Tapao to targets in Vietnam was so short that air-to-air refuelling was not normally required, and aircrew could work a normal day, with less than eight elapsed hours between pre-mission briefing and post strike debriefing, and with average sortie lengths of three hours or less.

U-Tapao was considerably upgraded and expanded to accommodate the B-52s, as only seven aircraft were initially able to fit onto the ramp, with eight more arriving after new concrete hard-

The 'boomer's eye view' of a B-52D, seen during a refuelling contact with a KC-135 tanker. Compared with the previous views of B-52Fs refuelling, this aircraft has new strips running fore and aft on the upper radome (*Robert F Dorr*)

standings had been quickly laid. The 15 aircraft at U-Tapao were still able to account for some 450 sorties per month out of the overall total of about 800 sorties per month.

The 15 U-Tapao-based aircraft came under the nominal control of the 4258th SW, which had been established in June 1966. Initially, they were restricted from operating against targets in Laos, or even overflying the nominally neutral country, but this restriction was lifted on 6 December 1967.

The U-Tapao aircraft were used during Operation *Neutralize* in September and October 1967. Some 820 *Arc Light* sorties were targeted against NVA artillery and infantry attempting to advance into South Vietnam during the Battle of Dak Tho. In September, 852 sorties were flown against NVA forces threatening the Marine Corps base at Con Thien, where the 'Buffs' inflicted no fewer than 3000 enemy casualties.

But such victories did little to influence the course of the war, and by 1968 it was reported that the B-52s had dropped a higher tonnage of bombs on Vietnam and Laos than the USAAF had dropped during the whole of World War 2. Whether or not this statistic was accurate, surprisingly little had been achieved. 'The enemy was elusive and all the bombers accomplished was to level huge stretches of jungle and kill lots of monkeys', remembered one former B-52 crewman.

COLOUR PLATES

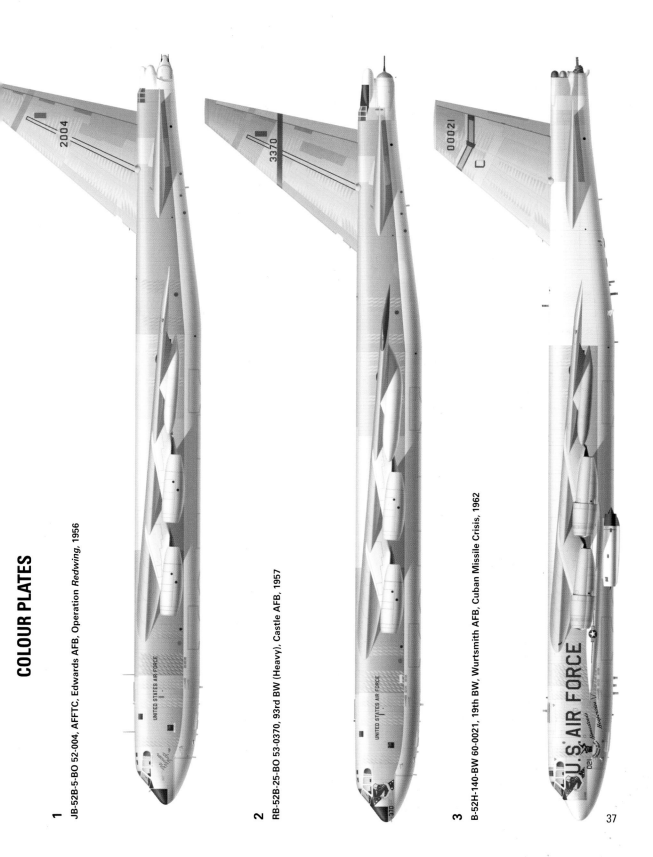

1
JB-52B-5-BO 52-004, AFFTC, Edwards AFB, Operation *Redwing*, 1956

2
RB-52B-25-BO 53-0370, 93rd BW (Heavy), Castle AFB, 1957

3
B-52H-140-BW 60-0021, 19th BW, Wurtsmith AFB, Cuban Missile Crisis, 1962

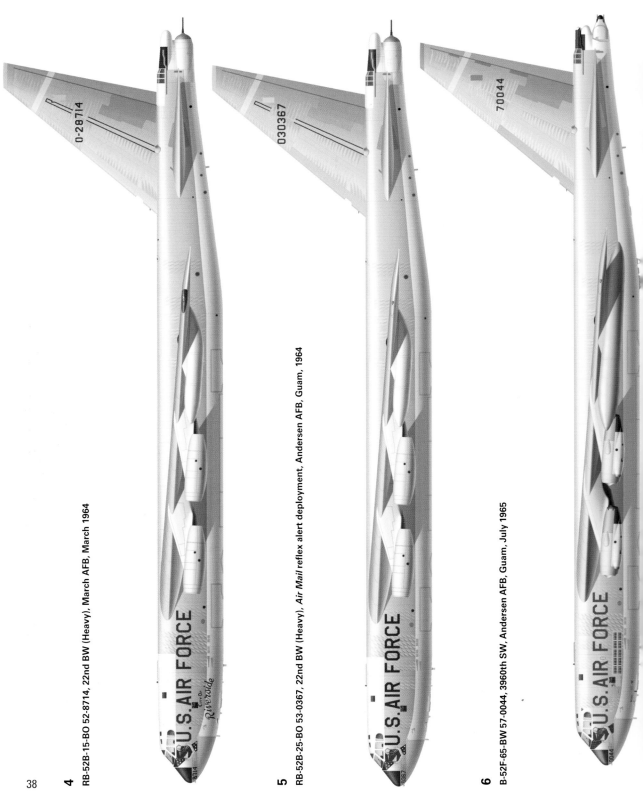

38

4
RB-52B-15-BO 52-8714, 22nd BW (Heavy), March AFB, March 1964

5
RB-52B-25-BO 53-0367, 22nd BW (Heavy), *Air Mail* reflex alert deployment, Andersen AFB, Guam, 1964

6
B-52F-65-BW 57-0044, 3960th SW, Andersen AFB, Guam, July 1965

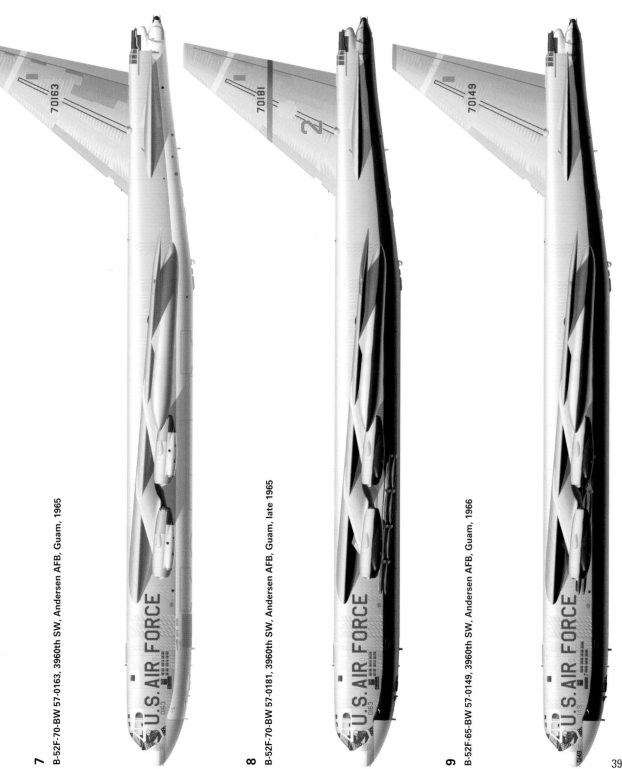

7

B-52F-70-BW 57-0163, 3960th SW, Andersen AFB, Guam, 1965

8

B-52F-70-BW 57-0181, 3960th SW, Andersen AFB, Guam, late 1965

9

B-52F-65-BW 57-0149, 3960th SW, Andersen AFB, Guam, 1966

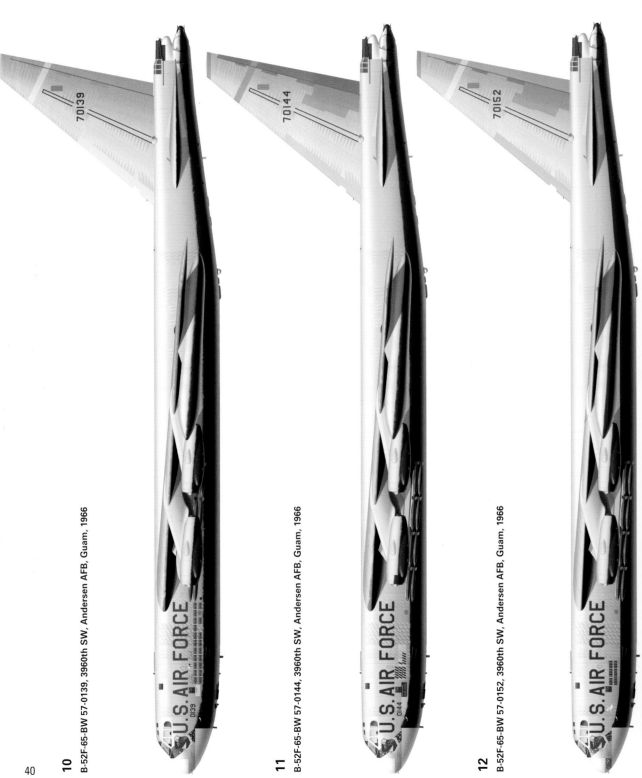

10 B-52F-65-BW 57-0139, 3960th SW, Andersen AFB, Guam, 1966

11 B-52F-65-BW 57-0144, 3960th SW, Andersen AFB, Guam, 1966

12 B-52F-65-BW 57-0152, 3960th SW, Andersen AFB, Guam, 1966

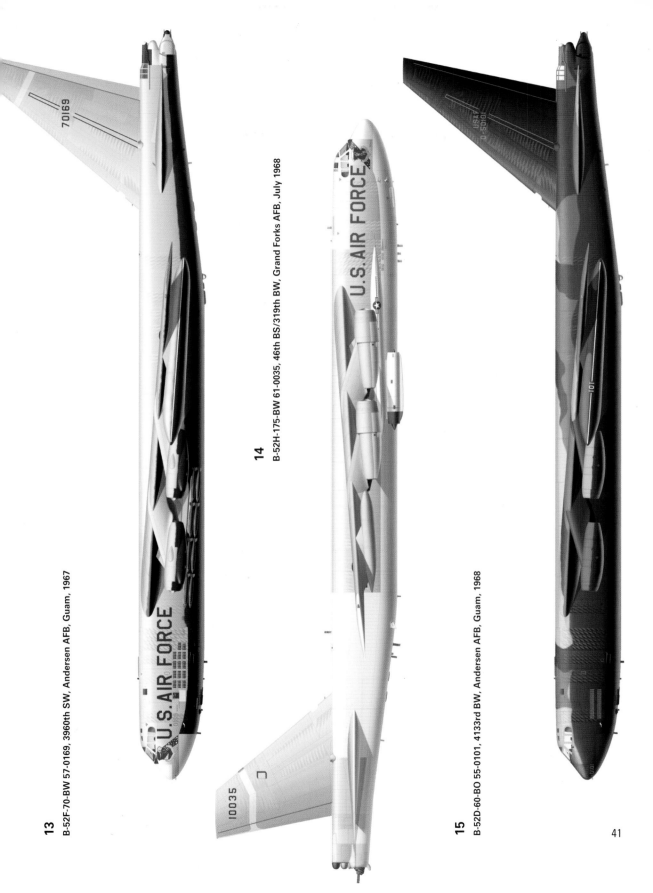

13
B-52F-70-BW 57-0169, 3960th SW, Andersen AFB, Guam, 1967

14
B-52H-175-BW 61-0035, 46th BS/319th BW, Grand Forks AFB, July 1968

15
B-52D-60-BO 55-0101, 4133rd BW, Andersen AFB, Guam, 1968

41

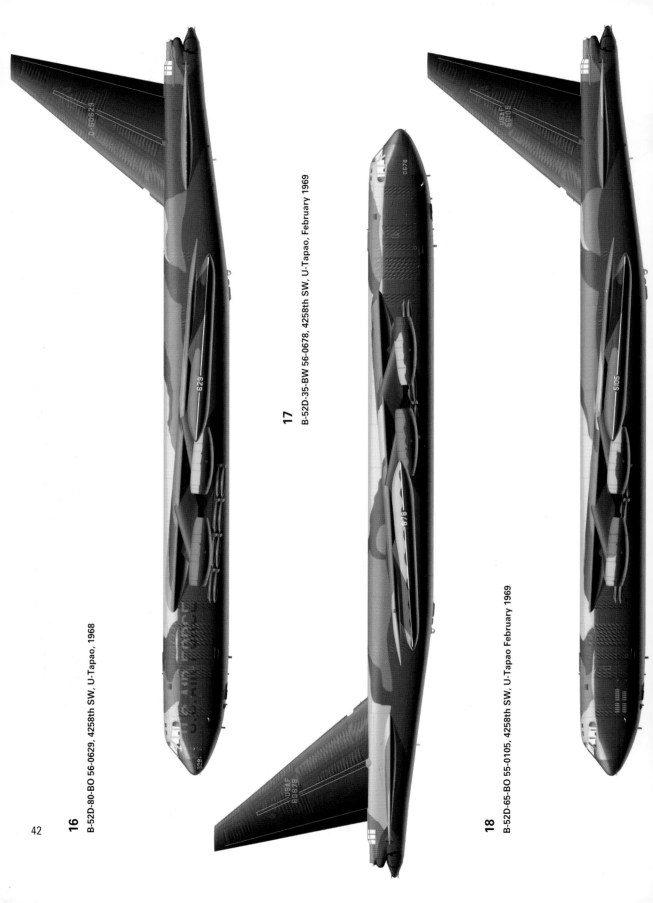

16
B-52D-80-BO 56-0629, 4258th SW, U-Tapao, 1968

17
B-52D-35-BW 56-0678, 4258th SW, U-Tapao, February 1969

18
B-52D-65-BO 55-0105, 4258th SW, U-Tapao February 1969

42

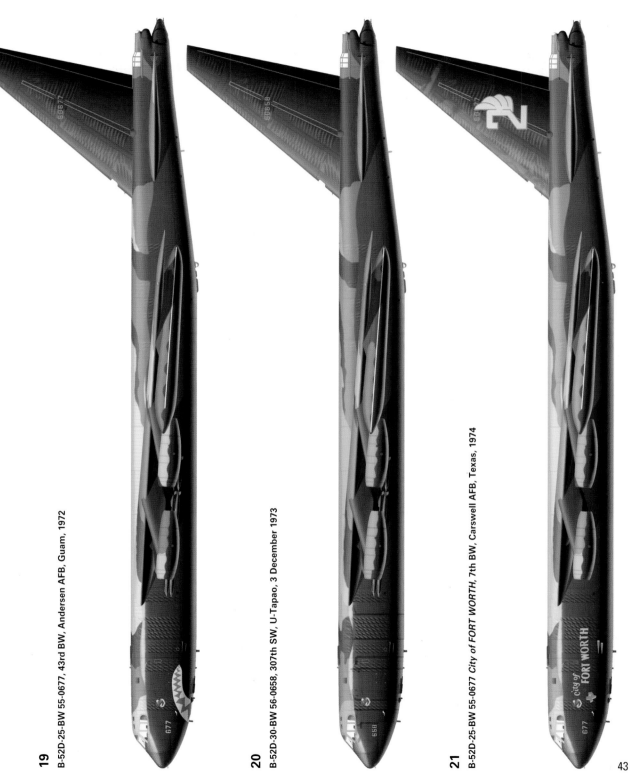

19

B-52D-25-BW 55-0677, 43rd BW, Andersen AFB, Guam, 1972

20

B-52D-30-BW 56-0658, 307th SW, U-Tapao, 3 December 1973

21

B-52D-25-BW 55-0677 *City of FORT WORTH*, 7th BW, Carswell AFB, Texas, 1974

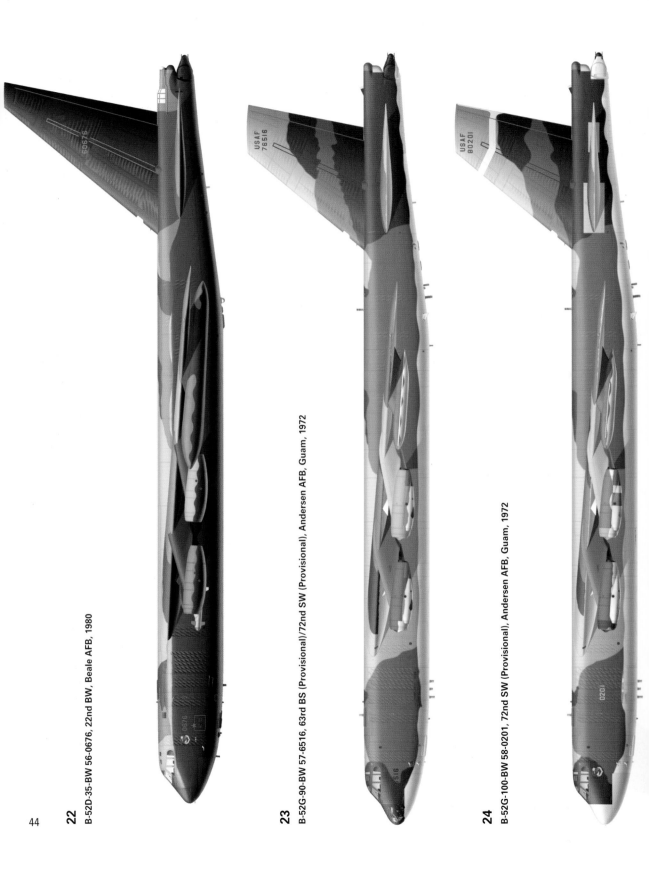

44

22

B-52D-35-BW 56-0676, 22nd BW, Beale AFB, 1980

23

B-52G-90-BW 57-6516, 63rd BS (Provisional)/72nd SW (Provisional), Andersen AFB, Guam, 1972

24

B-52G-100-BW 58-0201, 72nd SW (Provisional), Andersen AFB, Guam, 1972

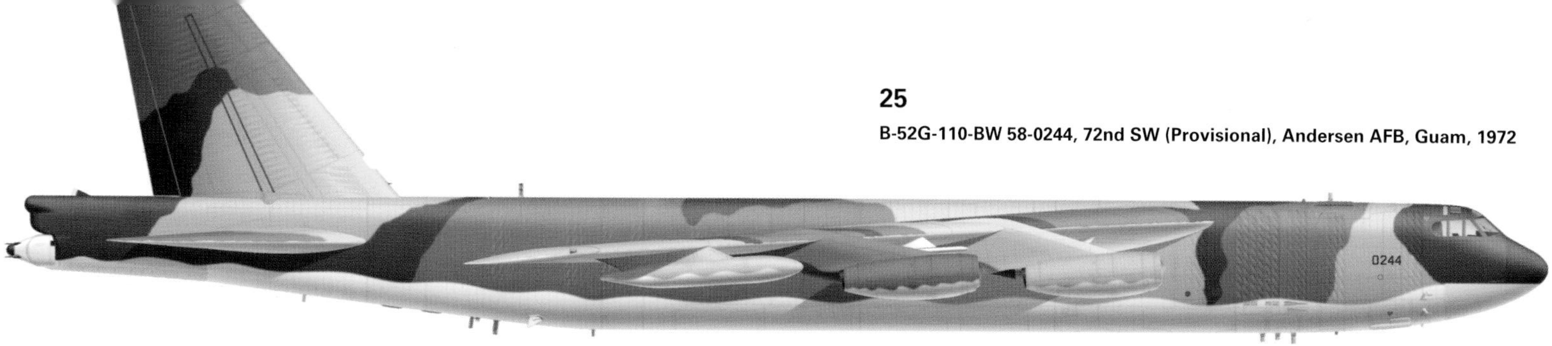

25

B-52G-110-BW 58-0244, 72nd SW (Provisional), Andersen AFB, Guam, 1972

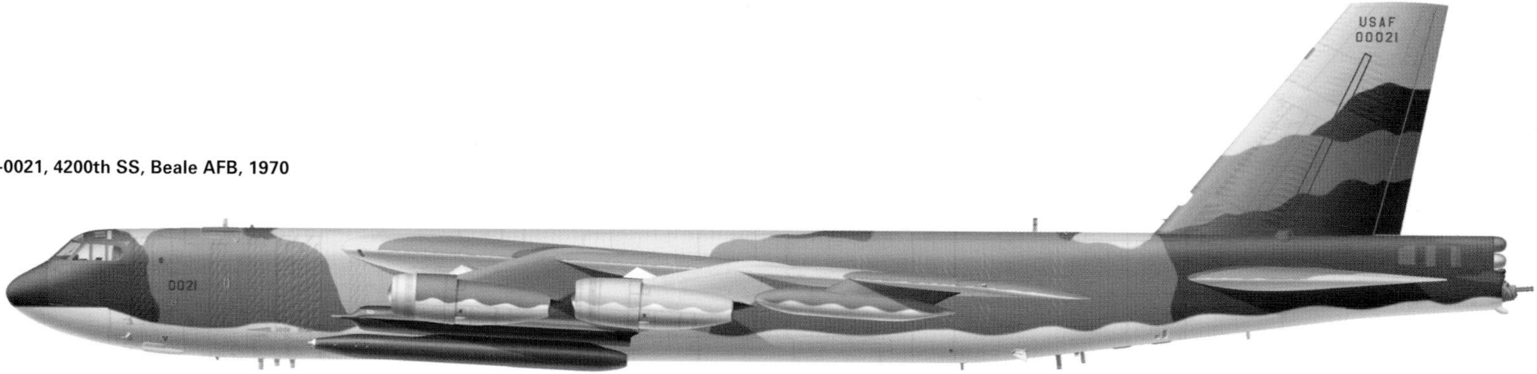

26

B-52H-140 60-0021, 4200th SS, Beale AFB, 1970

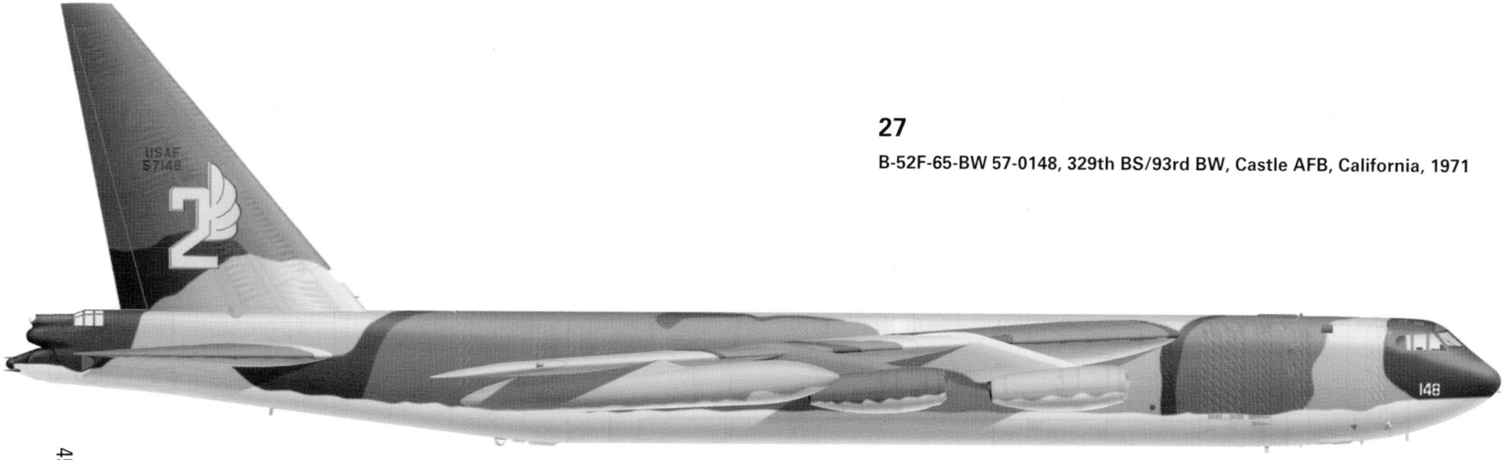

27

B-52F-65-BW 57-0148, 329th BS/93rd BW, Castle AFB, California, 1971

28

B-52G-95-BW 58-0174, 456th BW, Beale AFB, California, December 1973

29

B-52H-175-BW 61-0032, 17th BW, Wright Patterson AFB, Ohio, circa 1974

30

B-52G-120-BW 59-2569, 28th BW, Ellsworth AFB, 1976

ARC LIGHT CONTINUES

1968 opened with a desperate North Vietnamese attempt to win the war at a single stroke. The NVA launched a major offensive (the so-called Tet Offensive) which aimed to capture the main provincial capitals in South Vietnam, and to provoke an uprising by seizing and destroying the US Embassy in Saigon itself. Launched on 29 January during a 36-hour cease-fire for the Tet Lunar new year, the offensive involved huge numbers of regular NVA troops and South Vietnamese communist VC guerrillas. The offensive was beaten back with surprising ease, and represented a comprehensive military defeat for the communists. Only 318 US troops were killed, while NVA losses totalled 38,794 men killed and 6991 captured and the VC ceased to exist as a coherent and relevant independent force. This episode even served as a morale booster for the Army of the Republic of Vietnam (ARVN) and South Vietnamese police, and recruiting figures soared.

Fighting was perhaps fiercest in the ancient capital of Hue, where the NVA took the old city on 31 January, and were not finally defeated until 22 February. B-52s were not committed for fear of reducing the historic city to rubble, and the fighting was bitter and bloody. Seeing this on their television screens, the American public quickly realised that the war in Vietnam was far from being under control, and other events in 1968 only served to further this impression.

At the height of the Tet Offensive, North Vietnamese forces also made concerted efforts to capture the Marine base at Khe Sanh, 14 miles south of the DMZ and six miles from the Laotian border. The NVA eventually surrounded the three Marine and Vietnamese Ranger units (6000 troops) at Khe Sanh with a force of 30,000 NVA regulars and began conducting a methodical siege, building trenchworks that crept progressively closer and closer to the outpost. Air power would

B-52D-55-BO 55-0087 is seen taxiing back after a mission, its brake chute door still open, during 1968. The aircraft's serial was presented as O-50087 on the tail, using the short-lived O-for-obsolete prefix applied to aircraft which had been in service for more than ten years. Interestingly, the aircraft was still laden with bombs (*Robert F Dorr*)

prove crucial to the successful defence of Khe Sanh, both in resupplying the defenders and in directly attacking the NVA forces laying siege to the base.

Gen Westmoreland launched Operation *Niagara* on 14 January 1968, upping the B-52 sortie rate to 1800 per month, and ordering SAC to bomb the enemy forces, their staging and assembly areas and artillery positions. The B-52s dropped their bombs within 1700 yards of the base perimeter, even though the normal limit (with two *Skyspot* beacons) was 3300 yards from friendly forces. To maximise accuracy, the B-52s often descended to 24,000 ft in order to avoid the effects of high level winds. On a number of occasions the B-52Ds caught enemy troops in the open, and once killed 75 per cent of an 1800-man regiment. Then, on 19 March, some 1000 casualties were inflicted and a further 300 NVA troops deserted after a B-52 raid.

During the defence of Khe Sanh, from 15 February SAC began Operation *Bugle Call*, which saw a three-aircraft cell arrive at a designated pre-IP every 90 minutes, round the clock. From here a *Skyspot* operator could call the B-52s forward to a target. In practice, cells were compressed so that six bombers arrived at their pre-IP every three hours. The B-52s flew 461 missions, totalling 2707 sorties, and dropped 75,631 tons of bombs before the operation ended on 31 March. *Bugle Call* had contributed only 45 sorties out of the daily 300-sortie average, but had accounted for more than half of the ordnance expended. Westmoreland credited the B-52 with 'breaking the enemy's back'.

Monsoon weather had frequently grounded tactical aircraft, or prevented them from attacking their targets, whereas the B-52s, bombing by *Skyspot*, could operate round the clock, regardless of rain, mist or cloud. Because Khe Sanh was within range of SA-2 SAM batteries north of the DMZ, the B-52s operated with ECM support from *Tiny Tim* EB-66C/E jamming aircraft.

The high sortie rate demanded by the Khe Sanh operation was made possible by the opening of a third B-52 operating base. This was Kadena, on the Japanese island of Okinawa. Using the island for heavy bombers had hitherto been avoided in an effort to prevent causing offence to Japanese public opinion. It was, after all, only 20 years since USAF heavy bombers had devastated the Japanese homeland, some of them operating from the very bases which now housed the B-52 force.

The use of Kadena was finally authorised after North Korean forces seized the intelligence ship USS *Pueblo* on 23 January 1968, President

Much photographed and newly-painted B-52D-55-BO 55-0087 is seen here refuelling from a SAC KC-135A during Stateside training. This Stratotanker has the later, taller tailfin, which makes an interesting comparison with the tanker illustrated on page 24 (*Author's collection*)

B-52D-70-BO 56-0587 is towed back to its revetment at U-Tapao, the 'Buff's' underwing bomb racks empty after a successful mission. This aircraft survived the war, and was among the second batch of B-52Ds retired to the 'boneyard' in 1982-83 (*Robert F Dorr*)

Lyndon Johnson sending further forces to the region under Operation *Port Bow*, including 26 B-52Ds. Some 15 of the bombers joined the 4252nd SW at Kadena, while the remainder boosted numbers at Andersen AFB. Although Kadena was further from Saigon than U-Tapao, it was significantly closer than Andersen, and sortie duration was about six hours.

The beginning of B-52 operations from Kadena inaugurated a 30-month period during which B-52s operated from three bases in Southeast Asia.

Although the B-52D was the most numerous B-52 version then in service, it soon became clear that supporting the deployments at Andersen and U-Tapao would quickly over-stretch the force. After Gen Bruce K Holloway (a veteran of the 'Flying Tigers') took over SAC's reigns from Gen Joe Nazarro in 1968, aircrew from units flying other 'Buff' variants were finally included in the rotation, with individual crews from other wings, operating other B-52 versions, bulking out the deployed B-52D wing. This ensured that the onerous six-month combat tours were more evenly distributed throughout SAC, and helped to spread combat experience across all wings.

In fact, the combat tours were carefully set at 179 days, since an overseas posting of 180 days or more was deemed a 'permanent change of station', which was expensive and administratively more complex.

On 15 April 1968 a special Replacement Training Unit was established within the 93rd BW at Castle (the so-called 'Stratofortress School'), where crews from the B-52E, F, G or H underwent an intensive two-week 'D-Difference' course, which familiarised them with the 'idiosyncracies' of the older D-model. Those used to the later versions found the B-52D quite a handful, with heavier handling and a lack of power. It was 'like an 18-wheeler truck without power steering, airbrakes or automatic transmission in downtown Washington DC during the rush hour', according to one senior officer who sampled both types.

But heavier and less powerful did not mean more difficult. The G-model's short tailfin made it less stable, while the replacement of the ailerons with spoilers made the aircraft much lighter on the controls, and more difficult to fly precisely and accurately. Consequently, it took only four sorties to convert a crew onto the D-model. Once in theatre, crews underwent further training, learning role- and theatre-specific techniques and procedures with the SAC Contingency Aircrew Training (SCAT) School at Andersen AFB.

Even with these measures to spread the load, many B-52D crews found themselves flying 'six months on, six months off' in Southeast Asia, and SAC began to haemorrhage aircrew as people left for the airlines or sought transfers to other duties.

This view of B-52D-40-BW 56-0684 shows to advantage the 'faired in' tailgunner's cockpit. This gave its occupant no view directly aft (except through a periscope), but still proved useful for giving extra warning of approaching SAMs. Instead of an ejection seat, the whole back end of the turret could be jettisoned, allowing the gunner to simply 'step out'. In 11 B-52D incidents in 1972 which involved fatalities to any of the crew, four gunners were killed or MIA, compared with four pilots, two co-pilots, four navigators, seven EWOs and six radar navigators. This aircraft survived the war and served until the D-model was phased out (*Philip Jarrett*)

Highlights of the *Arc Light* campaign during 1968 included operations against bases in the A Shau valley, near the Laotian border, supporting the Army's Operation *Delaware* with 726 sorties. B-52Ds made their deepest penetration into North Vietnam on 14 July as part of Operation *Thor*, although they still ventured no further than 15 miles north of the DMZ. On 18 July B-52Ds attacked a SAM site in North Vietnam.

The *Rolling Thunder* bombing campaign against North Vietnam ended on 31 October, when President Johnson ordered an end to all air, naval and artillery bombardment of North Vietnam with effect from 0800 hrs the following morning. Johnson hoped to de-escalate the war and bring the North Vietnamese to the negotiating table, and wanted to be seen to be doing something 'big' before that year's Presidential elections.

Operations in South Vietnam and Laos continued, however, and these had always formed the bulk of the B-52's work in Southeast Asia. The B-52s had flown 35,680 sorties by November 1968, dropping 886,490 tons of bombs. Only 2380 of these sorties had been against North Vietnamese targets, which had also been attacked in 304,000 tactical sorties. The B-52s had flown 5217 *Arc Light*s in 1966 (including 650 over Laos and 280 over North Vietnam), 9686 in 1967 and an astounding 20,568 in 1968.

There were suggestions that tactical aircraft freed up by the end of *Rolling Thunder* could be used to replace the high profile B-52s, but MACV rejected this proposal, pointing out that a six-aircraft formation of B-52s could hit a two-kilometre-square target with 180 tons of bombs in only ten minutes, achieving an unmatched concentration of firepower. More than 100 tactical aircraft would be required to achieve something approaching the same result.

But American public support for the war was by now wavering, and incoming President Richard M Nixon publicly promised that he would disengage US forces from the war. The Nixon Administration actively and energetically built up South Vietnamese forces to be able to fight for themselves, while new US Secretary of State Henry Kissinger simultaneously pursued a diplomatic solution. In the meantime, however, US forces in-theatre continued to take the fight to the enemy. There was certainly little let-up for the B-52 crews, although there were changes.

Beating NVA and VC forces in South Vietnam was an uphill struggle, since it proved almost impossible to cut their supply lines, some of which came through neighbouring neutral countries. The campaign against targets in Laos has already been described, but from 18 March 1969, a new country joined the target list. Following a request from new MACV commander Creighton Adams, Nixon secretly authorised B-52 bombing raids on enemy bases in Cambodia.

The Cambodian raids were initially kept secret, and records were falsified to show that the targets attacked had been in South Vietnam. Because the missions were conducted at night, under radar control, many B-52 crewmen also 'believed' that they were simply attacking targets in South Vietnam. The Cambodian bombing campaign lasted until 16 August 1973, although it was carried out in the open after April 1970, when Cambodia was invaded following the overthrow of Prince Norodom Sihanouk.

This cell of three heavily weathered aircraft, led by B-52D-5-BW 55-0054, was photographed taxiing back at U-Tapao during October 1968. The lead 'Buff' was retired to the 'boneyard' in late 1978. Unit markings and mission tallies were rarely applied to the B-52Ds (*Robert F Dorr*)

Some 3630 *Arc Light* sorties were flown in the first year of the operation (dropping 100,000 tons of bombs on neutral Cambodia), and the eventual total reached 16,500. The raids did a great deal to destabilise Cambodia's government, and may have helped create the conditions under which the Khmer Rouge would eventually seize control.

During the two-month US invasion, which saw ground forces penetrate some 18 miles into Cambodia to destroy NVA, VC and Khmer Rouge forces and facilities, the B-52s flew 763 sorties, and crews reported seeing the biggest secondary explosions they had ever encountered when they bombed suspected weapons dumps and bases.

Nor did operations in Laos ease up. During 1970, Operation *Good Look* saw intensive bombing missions flown against NVA forces as they prepared for an offensive in the Plain of Jars.

But overall, the effort did slacken slightly from its peak during late 1968, with the monthly sortie rate dropping to 1600 on 18 July 1969 and to 1400 on 6 October. A further cut, to 1000 sorties per month, was made on 16 August 1970.

Five B-52s had been lost during 1965-67, and five more would be destroyed during 1968-69. None were the result of enemy action, and – unlike the initial spate of accidents – all of the aircraft were lost at or near their deployment bases. On 18 November 1968 306th BW B-52D 55-0103 aborted its take off from Kadena, but left the decision too late and ran off the end of the runway, where it caught fire. The ECM operator was burned to death, but the rest of the crew evacuated the blazing aircraft. An almost identical accident befell 70th BW B-52D 55-0676 at U-Tapao on 19 July 1969. This time all of the crew escaped from the aircraft, but the base HH-43 rescue helicopter was destroyed when the aircraft exploded and its bombload 'cooked off'.

Another 306th BW B-52D (55-0115) was destroyed in a ground fire at Kadena on 3 December 1968, and the remaining two aircraft crashed into the sea after take off from Andersen. 56-0593, of the 509th BW, was lost on 10 May 1969, crashing into the sea soon after take off from Andersen, while 56-0630 of the 70th BW suffered a starboard wing failure soon after taking off from the base on 27 July 1969.

From April 1970, the B-52 deployments at Andersen and U-Tapao had been staffed in a new way. Instead of deploying whole bomb wings from CONUS, SAC sent individual crews out for a six-month tour. They spent 17 weeks at Andersen, and the remainder of their time at U-Tapao. The Thai base had been converted from simple FOL to a full base in January 1969 with the addition of new permanent buildings and facilities in place of tents and trailers. The ramp area had also been expanded, resulting in more B-52 revetments.

The growth of B-52 operations at U-Tapao also stimulated the establishment of a nearby 'Boom Town' of bars and brothels, including the infamous 'Yellow Balloon', where the girls charged bored B-52 personnel 50 baht (about $5US) for as much fun as they could handle. This was principally recreation for the groundcrews, since while a dose of the 'clap' was inconvenient for them, it could prove fatal for a pilot if he was shot down and incarcerated (with no means of getting treatment) by the North Vietnamese.

The B-52D force in-theatre was drawn down during 1970, with operations at Andersen (where the 4133rd had been replaced by the new 43rd SW on 1 July) and Kadena slowing to a trickle as the pace of operations at U-Tapao built up to handle an eventual total of 42 B-52Ds. In September 1970, 'Buff' combat operations were halted at Anderson and Kadena, with *Arc Light* continuing exclusively from U-Tapao. The Third Air Division, meanwhile, was deactivated, its place being taken by the Eighth Air Force, now headquartered at Andersen.

The 43rd SW at Andersen had become part of SAC's alert force on 16 August, and apart from the fact that all departing crews pulled one week on alert at Andersen before going back Stateside, Andersen was remote from the war in Vietnam. Even the SCAT School for aircrew arriving 'in-theatre' was transferred to U-Tapao.

1971 saw another intensive series of attacks in the Laotian pan handle, supporting ARVN troops as they tried to stop traffic along the Ho Chi Minh Trail during Operation *Lam Son 719*.

The B-52s frequently dropped their bombs within 300 yards of friendly troops, such was the confidence in their accuracy. Enemy casualties were heavy, estimated at more than 1700. Between 8 February and 24 March the B-52s flew 1358 sorties and dropped 32,000 tons of bombs, with the monthly sortie rate climbing back to 1200.

By the beginning of 1972, it had become clear that a major NVA offensive was being prepared, with traffic along the Ho Chi Minh trail having reached record levels as men and material poured southwards. MACV requested B-52 strikes to stem the flow, and on 8 February the B-52 sortie rate was upped to 1200 per month, and a new B-52 build-up effort – Operation *Bullet Shot* – was quickly launched, preparing the ground for a new and more bloody phase in the B-52's war in Southeast Asia.

The characteristic nose-down attitude of the 'Buff' on take off is well shown in this view of B-52D-30-BW 56-0663 departing Kadena in February 1968. The B-52's bicycle undercarriage prevented a normal 'rotate' on take off, and the aircraft was held level (slightly nose down) and climbed due to the incidence of the wing, rather than deliberate pilot input! *(Robert F Dorr)*

FREEDOM TRAIN AND *LINEBACKER*

President Nixon's policy of 'Vietnamization' was put to the test on 30 March 1972, when the North Vietnamese invaded South Vietnam. US officials had been predicting that the South would 'soon be able to defend itself' for some time, although many believed that this was a shallow justification for US disengagement, rather than a realistic assessment of the military situation. On 10 December 1971 Nixon made an impotent warning that North Vietnam would be bombed if it escalated the fighting while US troop withdrawals took place, and then on 13 January 1972 announced that 70,000 US troops would be withdrawn, leaving only 69,000 behind. This was all crowd-pleasing stuff for the US electorate during an election year, but was interpreted by Hanoi as a massive display of weakness and indecision.

The massive offensive, supported by artillery and tanks, was primarily opposed by South Vietnamese ARVN units, with US tactical air power in-country being limited to three F-4 squadrons and a single unit with A-37 Dragonflies. There was an immediate reinforcement effort, sending TAC fighter-bomber units to bases in South Korea and Thailand under Operation *Constant Guard*.

At the same time, SAC reinforced the 50 B-52Ds left at U-Tapao through a series of *Bullet Shot* deployments, which saw huge numbers of B-52s returning to Andersen AFB on Guam, where a handful of 60th BS B-52Ds had been standing nuclear alert duty. At the beginning of 1972, U-Tapao had housed 42 B-52Ds, but eight more had been deployed to the base on 5 February, in recognition of increased NVA infiltration, and in expectation of the invasion.

This minor increase was followed by five numbered *Bullet Shot* deployments. Under *Bullet.Shot I*, on 7 February 1972, the reinforce-

With the urgent requirement to deploy aircraft to Southeast Asia for *Freedom Train*, some aircraft arrived in-theatre already in urgent need of a repaint. Round-the-clock flying in tropical conditions soon caused the external finish of such aircraft to deteriorate even more. This Andersen-based B-52D-60-BO (55-0101) was particularly well-worn, with large areas of dull and matted paint. The aircraft had its 'last three' ('101') in white hastily painted over the remains of the 'last four' ('red 0101') in red (*Robert F Dorr*)

ments included 29 B-52Ds from the 7th BW at Carswell, the 96th BW at Dyess and the 306th BW at McCoy. *Bullet Shot II*, on 4 April, saw the despatch of another 22 B-52Ds from the 22nd BW at March and the 99th BW from Westover. Six more B-52Ds from these two units deployed to Guam on 8 April as *Bullet Shot IIA*.

On 11 April, SAC launched *Bullet Shot III*, and for the first time the B-52Ds were augmented by newer B-52Gs. Some 28 of the latter were rushed out to Southeast Asia from the 2nd BW at Barksdale during 10-16 April, with five more following on 6 May and seven on 21 May under *Bullet Shot IV*. This brought the number of B-52s at Andersen to 140 aircraft. The final phase of the reinforcement effort was instituted on 23 May, with the addition of a further 58 B-52Gs.

The G-model was not nearly so well suited for active duty as was the B-52D, since it could not carry bombs underwing, and lacked the *Big Belly* modifications that had given the B-52D its formidable load-carrying capability. The aircraft could thus carry only 27 bombs – about one quarter of the D-model's payload.

Moreover, while some B-52Gs assigned to conventional warfare missions had been given the same *Rivet Rambler*, or Phase V, ECM electronic warfare updates as the B-52D during 1967-69, the type did not generally have quite so comprehensive an ECM fit as the older version. There was, however, little alternative to this deployment, since the B-52D force had been reduced by attrition, while all B-52B, Cs and Es, and many of the B-52Fs, had been retired.

Some of the B-52Gs that went through the *Rivet Rambler*/Phase V ECM upgrade programme were also fitted with hardpoints for the carriage of AN/ALE-25 forward-firing chaff dispenser rocket pods (containing 20 Tracor AN/ADR-8 2.5-inch folding fin chaff rockets)

B-52G 58-0182 was used as a test aircraft for defensive systems, and is pictured here, in February 1965, with an ALE-25 chaff rocket pod (subsequently used by operational G-models) underwing. The aircraft also tested engine exhaust shields, which were not adopted more widely. 58-0182 was later returned to the frontline, and even went on to fight in *Desert Storm*, flying eight missions as *What's Up Doc*. It was finally retired from the 379th BW on 10 June 1992 (*Author's collection*)

between the engine pods. These pylons allowed the carriage of other defensive systems, and some Guam-based B-52Gs were fitted with AN/ALQ-119(V) ECM pods in place of the AN/ALE-25 chaff pods.

The full B-52 force deployed for use in Vietnam in 1972 was bigger than at any time in the past, and represented well over one-third of the active fleet. At this time, the B-52 force still represented arguably the most important leg of the Strategic Nuclear Triad, with ICBMs and SLBMs, and the loss of B-52s for combat in Vietnam placed great strain on the USA's strategic deterrent.

With about 153 B-52s at Andersen (55 B-52Ds and 98 B-52Gs), all operated by a single wing (the 43rd), a major administrative reorganisation took place on 1 June. The 57th Air Division (Provisional) was established as an intermediate layer below the Eighth Air Force HQ, controlling the 303rd Consolidated Aircraft Maintenance Wing, the 43rd SW (Provisional) and the 72nd SW (Provisional). The 43rd SW controlled two provisional bomb squadrons of B-52Ds, (the 60th and 63rd) while the 72nd SW (Provisional) controlled four provisional squadrons of B-52Gs (the 64th, 65th, 329th and 486th BSs).

The huge number of aircraft deployed to Andersen far exceeded the number of available parking spaces, but this problem was solved by the simple expedient of ensuring that at least 30 aircraft (about 20 per cent of the force) were airborne at any one time. With missions lasting at least 12 hours, this was less difficult than it sounds! At one time it had been hoped to station some of the B-52s at Kadena, but Okinawa was to be handed back to Japanese control on 15 May 1972, and local sensitivities meant that only tankers and support types (and certainly not heavy bombers) could be based there. The base was occasionally used as an emergency diversion, however.

This B-52G was painted in an experimental tan and green camouflage scheme, perhaps with Southeast Asia in mind. In the event, though, B-52Gs that deployed to Vietnam were operated in their standard Single Integrated Operational Plan (SIOP) camouflage (*Author's collection*)

At U-Tapao, the new 17th Air Division (Provisional) controlled the 307th SW, with two squadrons of about 50 B-52Ds (the 364th and 365th BSs). U-Tapao accounted for the bulk of the bomb tonnage delivered by the B-52 force, since all of its aircraft were *Big Belly* B-52Ds – these aircraft could also fly a mission in less than three hours. Three-quarters of the aircraft at far away Andersen were B-52Gs, which carried one-quarter of the bombload, although with their higher maximum take-off weight (488,000 lbs rather than 450,000 lbs) they could also carry full fuel, and could make the round trip from Guam without refuelling.

Bob Thompson was a young B-52D co-pilot who deployed to Andersen from Westover AFB under *Bullet Shot*;

'The 99th BW got the word to go with all 16 of our D-models, and as many tankers as we could scrape together. The CO asked "When?" and I guess the answer was "Yesterday", because they even diverted one aeroplane in flight, while it was flying to depot at Kelly AFB for maintenance and a much needed re-paint. They even had one of the maintenance officers on board. Man, he must have been surprised when they landed – he'd expected to step out into the Texan sunshine and ended up in the rain at Guam!

'Several of our aircraft should have been overhauled and repainted before hitting the war zone – flying through that monsoon rain beat the hell out of the paintwork, and the 99th's jets soon looked like a fleet of Bolivian meat-haulers. One jet was completely matted, and always got written up for excessive fuel consumption – and the engineer's serious response was always that the aeroplane needed a repaint.'

'I wished that we'd been sent to U-Tapao, where they flew much shorter missions (they were much closer to the targets), and where they seemed to work at a more leisurely place. And if they did get some leave, they were in Thailand, with lots to see. Just our luck to be sent to a volcanic rock in the middle of the Pacific, which dictated that every sortie was more than half-a-day long! At U-Tapao, their 50 aircraft were tasked with flying 39 sorties per day, while at Andersen our 153 aircraft were expected to mount 66 daily sorties.

'It all followed a pretty rigid pattern, with the jets departing in 22 "ballgames" (three-aircraft cells), each with a standard load-out – 42 M117s internal and 24 Mk 82s external. The whole point of the D-model was that you could load it more easily with pre-loaded "C" clips of bombs, and I believe they used clips at U-Tapao, but at Andersen the armourers did it the old fashioned way. I don't know why. Maybe it was to make sure there were the fewest possible differences between how the armourers had to work on the D- and the G-models, because the latter couldn't use clips at all.

'The B-52Gs flew much lighter, with 27 M117s in the bomb-bay only, so were carrying 15 fewer bombs internally, and didn't carry anything under the wing at all. We used to play the G guys up about that whenever the opportunity arose, and termed them "light bombardment"! But the two types were operated quite separately, and I don't really know how they went about their business. I just know that our 43rd SW provided just shy of half of the daily "ballgames", while the 72nd (controlling the Gs) provided the rest.

'For each B-52D "ballgame" the maintainers prepared five jets – three primaries, a primary spare and a secondary "spare" spare. The fifth sat it out preflighted and ready to go, but was not crewed up. The three primary jets and the first spare were all fully preflighted, armed and crewed up, and all four started engines about three-quarters-of-an-hour before "go"! It took about 30-45 minutes to preflight the jet and to load up all the gear, and whenever we could, we factored in enough time to just relax under the wing for ten minutes before we strapped in. That gave enough time for some of the sweat to dry out of your flightsuit.

'If there was a problem with any of the three primary aircraft, its crew would race to the primary spare, and the spare crew would decant to the "spare" spare and start up its engines. The spare crew would only launch if one of the primaries went u/s while taxiing or during take-off (or shortly after).

'Getting airborne with all three jets in a cell was important, not only because a cell of three aircraft had proved to be the best way of concentrating bombs in a given box on the ground, but also because it allowed the onboard ECM equipment to be used to the best possible effect, ensuring all round coverage and maximising and concentrating jamming power.

'Up until that point in the war, the B-52 had flown milk runs. One guy had been fired at by an SA-2 battery back in 1965 or 1966, but apart from that, it had been straightforward. Out from Guam (or U-Tapao or Kadena if you were lucky), knock down some trees, kill some monkeys (or do something really helpful for the "Grunts" if you were lucky) and then home for "tea and medals". But that all changed during *Linebacker*. Suddenly, we were being sent so far north that we were flying over the "badlands", where the enemy actually had SAMs ready and waiting.

'Before 1972, it seemed that the B-52s avoided North Vietnamese airspace wherever possible, and when we did fly north of the border, we only flew a few miles north of the DMZ. And when the intelligence boys decided that there might be SA-2s within range of a certain spot, we didn't go back there. Shooting down a B-52s would have been a propaganda victory for North Vietnam, and would have been

Bristling with EW antennas under the rear fuselage, this B-52D-35-BW (56-0674) went on to become the last B-52D to be retired by the USAF, flying to MASDC on 4 October 1983. The last D-model to fly an operational mission had been 'MiG killer' 56-0676, which had flown back to the US from Andersen three days earlier. The last B-52D to fly, however, was 56-0687, which was briefly stored at Carswell AFB and then flown to Florida for display on 20 February 1984 (Robert F Dorr)

embarrassing to the State Department, so the risk wasn't taken. And that was fine by me! But in *Linebacker* all that changed, and suddenly Nixon didn't seem to mind so much if the NVA downed a "Buff" or two. I didn't regard that as being progress, personally, and I felt that I was doing more than enough to earn my $65 per month Combat Pay, and my $1 per day separation allowance!

'As if to hammer the lesson home, one guy had been hit by a SAM on the first mission in April, and SAM firings became more and more common. They gave you an Air Medal after 20 *Arc Light*s – or after ten missions "up North", where each mission counted for two.

'Even without the NVA trying to shoot you in the ass, B-52 operations were dangerous. With *Pacer Plank* they'd structurally strengthened the "Buff", but there were still worries about fatigue, and everyone knew that at least a couple of aircraft had broken up in the air, so that was always at the back of your mind – especially operating at the very heavy weights we were used to during *Linebacker*.

'But from Guam, we were just operating at the absolute limit weight wise, taxiing out way above maximum take off weight, relying on fuel burn and using the water to get down to weight, and using the overrun at both ends of the runway. Every take-off used water injection, but even so, you were usually on the end of the runway by the time you got to V2 (unstick), and it might take five minutes, sometimes more, to reach your climb speed of 280 knots.

'Just to remind you of how marginal it could be, you'd often here the patter of stones and debris hitting the aircraft as you hit the gravel at the end of the runway. Sometimes you lost height after going over the cliff, and I believe that at least one B-52 actually hit the water. It must have felt like an eternity for those on the downward-firing ejection seats, who needed a 700-ft minimum altitude to bale out.

'Over the target, I was buoyed by the knowledge that no B-52 had been shot down, although that did not stop me from observing the requirement to fly faster (470 knots, rather than 450) in known threat areas. What did worry me was that we seemed to make no effort to be anything other than predictable. We usually all attacked from the same direction, using the same altitudes and the same departure headings, and arrived over the target at predictable intervals. As if that were not quite obvious enough, we had to test the ECM and the chaff dispensers at a set distance before the target.

'Even without the worry posed by enemy defences, there were plenty of things in a mission which could quickly spoil your day. We were flying in some very unfavourable weather conditions, and systems failures (inevitable on hard-worked aircraft of that age, in those days) could make it extremely difficult. On one occasion our radar failed and we had to fly what we called a "bonus deal" – flying the mission in trail, with the gunner in the aircraft ahead using his radar to position us. The radio got plenty busy, but the technique worked extremely well.

'Then on the way back the fatigue would kick in, and tiredness became a real enemy, although fuel was always critical, and I found that quite a useful aid to staying alert!'

'If things were hard for the aircrews on Guam, it was much tougher for the troops. At the end of the day, there were just too many personnel for the base to support, and too many folk had to live in the "Tin City" of steel dormitories. The unlucky ones had to endure the hell that was "Canvas Court" – a sprawling tent city with no hot water, inadequate sanitation and all in tropical heat and humidity. The Base Flight Surgeon was shipped out when he reported the reality of conditions, because it was more convenient for the "brass" to believe that everything was okay, but asthma and other respiratory problems became endemic as people slept on damp and mouldy mattresses, and we must have come close to a cholera outbreak.

'I always wondered why they didn't use Kadena again, until we had to divert there after we lost an engine on the way back from a mission. Local protestors reacted as though we'd launched an unprovoked A-bomb attack from Japanese soil. God knows what the reaction would have been if we'd flown bombing operations from the base.'

Even as the B-52 force began to build up at the two bases, close air support sorties aimed at blunting the North Vietnamese invasion had been authorised on 2 April, under the codename *Freedom Train*, but these proved less than completely successful. Long-standing restrictions against attacking targets inside North Vietnam were therefore lifted on 9 April (after extending the 'bombing line' from the 17th parallel to the 18th on 4 April and then to the 19th two days later). The USAF immediately began a campaign of interdiction against the NVA's supply lines and military infrastructure, and the communist advance began to stall. These were the first cross border attacks since the end of Operation *Rolling Thunder*, on 31 October 1968.

For the first time in the war, Washington was quick to permit the geographical scope of air operations to be expanded, and was much more willing to leave target selection and other military decisions to the military commanders on the ground. Targets which had been 'off limits' since the beginning of the US involvement were now added to the approved target list. This was in marked contrast to how the Johnson administration had 'handled' the war. President Johnson and his defence secretary, Robert S MacNamara, had imposed impractical and sometimes absurd 'rules of engagement', frequently micro-managing the conduct of the war and failing to delegate decisions, thus handicapping US forces as they tried to win the war.

MacNamara displayed a withering contempt for many senior officers, and obstinately refused to listen to advice. Tactics were artificially limited and constrained in an insane effort to avoid escalating the war

By the end of the USAF involvement in the Vietnam War, the B-52s had adopted an extremely anonymous appearance. Small SAC badges appeared under the port side of the cockpit on some aircraft, but wing badges remained rare. SAC also frowned upon displays of individualism like nose art, aircraft names or bomb logs. This B-52D-35-BW (56-0671) remained in service at Andersen after the war, finally retiring in 1982-83 (*Robert F Dorr*)

This smart-looking aircraft (B-52D-60-BO 55-0095) ended its life as a ground instructional airframe at Chanute AFB, Illinois, after long and distinguished service in Vietnam. The introduction of new polyurethane paint in the early 1970s made the B-52D's camouflage finish much more durable (*Robert F Dorr*)

or offending the enemy! Nor was there any consistency, and there was never a coherent or effective military or political strategy beyond a continuing effort to force the North Vietnamese to negotiate, while avoiding any escalation in the war.

The Nixon Administration still insisted that the avoidance of collateral damage should be accorded an important priority, but otherwise left much more of the conduct of the war to the generals.

The first B-52 raid of the campaign was mounted on 9 April, when 15 B-52Ds attacked railway yards and oil storage facilities at Vinh. One of the aircraft was hit, losing most of one underwing tank, but the B-52D recovered safely to Da Nang. Three days later, 18 B-52s hit the airfields at Bai Thuong and, over the weekend of 15-16 April, POL targets near Hanoi (North Vietnam's capital) and Haiphong (its main port) were attacked, drawing up 35 SAMs. None of these hit their targets, however, thanks to masterful defence suppression efforts by a fleet of *Wild Weasels* and *Iron Hand* suppression aircraft.

`Another 18 B-52Ds hit railway facilities and a power plant at Than Hoa on 21 and 23 April, triggering the launch of 50 SAMs. One of the B-52Ds (56-0665, flown by Capt Alward) was hit by a SAM, suffering the loss of two engines. Despite being peppered by 400 shrapnel fragments (which caused multiple fuel leaks), the aircraft limped to Da Nang. With two engines out on one side, and the other two failing, Alward made a hot and high approach, touching down halfway along the runway. When the brake 'chute failed to deploy, he went around again and finally landed safely. The aircraft was eventually repaired and returned to service.

On 10 May Operation *Freedom Train* was renamed, somewhat clumsily, *Rolling Thunder Alpha*, before the name of the operation against North Vietnam was changed again, later that day, to Operation *Linebacker*.

Despite this bomber activity, the NVA forces quickly captured the provincial capital of Quang Tri, and besieged An Loc and Kontum. At Quang Tri, B-52s ensured that the NVA victory was a costly won, killing 300 soldiers in one raid and destroying 35 advancing tanks in another. At Kontum, 2262 B-52 *Arc Lights* undertaken between 16 May and 6 June hit 795 targets around the city, preventing the NVA from taking it. A further 254 *Arc Lights* helped save An Loc, performing a crucial role, and in the Central Highlands *Arc Light* sorties repelled massive enemy assaults.

The local commander, Gen McGiffert, later observed that;

'The B-52 was the most effective weapon we have been able to muster, and was absolutely central to the successful defence effort against the invading force. Its massive firepower made the crucial difference in such key areas as An Loc and Kontum.'

By 29 June, Nixon was able to record that, 'The situation has been completely turned around. The South Vietnamese are now on the offensive', and the Paris Peace Talks resumed on 13 July, as US and South Vietnamese forces continued to drive back the NVA.

Operations against targets in the north continued throughout the summer of 1972, concentrating on the rail links between Vietnam and its principal source of weapons, China. The *Linebacker* missions accounted for only 10-18 per cent of the overall B-52 effort, however, which remained primarily focused on *Arc Light* sorties in the south and in neighbouring countries.

Even after the North Vietnamese offensive was halted, and all NVA forces had been chased back across the border (by about 26 June, when enemy forces quit An Loc), the *Linebacker* and *Arc Lights* raids continued at an intensive pace. Under such concerted pressure, the North Vietnamese negotiating team in Paris began to adopt a more positive tone in the long-running peace talks. The sortie rate dipped in October, before the US Presidential election, and when breakthrough in the Peace Talks appeared imminent.

This was the time for the USA to assert its superiority and enforce a peace settlement from a position of strength. Instead, on 22 October, Nixon and his National Security Advisor Henry Kissinger made an ill-judged concession, calling off all air operations above the 20th parallel. This effectively placed Hanoi and Haiphong 'off limits' to US air power, and gave the North Vietnamese an invaluable breathing space during which air defences (virtually destroyed during *Linebacker*) could be repaired and reorganised and strengthened.

In the face of the concession, North Vietnamese leader Le Duc Tho decided that the war should be continued in the hope that further ground would be ceded by the US side, and while supply lines, troop strengths and military units were rebuilt and strengthened. Although the North Vietnamese announced that they had reached agreement with the US on a nine point peace plan on 26 October, the Paris peace negotiations continued to falter and stutter, and it became increasingly clear that the USA was not going to achieve the 'Peace with Honour' (with a return of US PoWs and some guarantees of South Vietnamese security) which it sought.

On 22 November the B-52 force suffered its first combat loss to enemy action. A U-Tapao based B-52D (55-0110) was hit by a SAM during a raid on Vinh. The B-52D was badly damaged, but pilot Capt Norbert J Ostrozny from the 96th BW at Dyess was determined not to fall into enemy hands, and managed to turn the crippled bomber on course for the Thai border, hoping to limp the 400 miles back to base. The bomber lost height as it struggled south, with the engines continually failing as more of the wing fuel was consumed.

Finally, some 100 miles from the target, at 15,000 ft, as the aircraft crossed the border, the starboard wingtip broke away and Ostrozny

was forced to give the order to bale out from the burning bomber. Fortunately, a CH-53 on a night reconnaissance from Nakhon Phanom was already in the area, and the crew were spotted while they descended in their parachutes, and were recovered safely by the helicopter, and a Kaman 'Pedro', within moments of landing. Pilot Ostrozny won the Silver Star in recognition of his determination and courage. The aircraft was the 11th B-52 lost in Southeast Asia to all causes, in 100,000 sorties.

Ill-judged North Vietnamese celebration at the shoot-down played into the hands of US 'Hawks', and it was suddenly easy to present the North Vietnamese as being aggressive, confrontational and determined to continue the military struggle, while pressure to teach the Vietnamese a lesson grew steadily more intense.

The Nixon Administration finally lost patience with the peace negotiations at the end of 1972, and realised that a more forceful approach would be required, as Kissinger later explained. 'It was decided to try to bring home that the continuation of the war had its price'. When the North Vietnamese broke off negotiations on 13 December, Nixon therefore ordered an all-out air offensive against North Vietnam. The President privately noted that 'Those bastards have never been bombed like they're going to be bombed this time!' and *Linebacker II* was born.

This particular B-52D-65-BO (55-0110) was the first 'Buff' to be lost to enemy action during the Vietnam War. The aircraft was hit by an SA-2 during a raid on Vinh on 22 November 1972, although its pilot, Capt Norbert J 'Oz' Ostrozny, kept the bomber under control and turned for home. He managed to limp all the way to the Thai border, where a large portion of the starboard wingtip broke off, and he ordered the crew to bale out. All were recovered safely by nearby helicopters, and Ostrozny was subsequently awarded a Silver Star (*Robert F Dorr*)

LINEBACKER II

B y early December 1972, it was clear that the Paris Peace Talks would not succeed, and that the North Vietnamese would not become any less intransigent without significant further pressure. Accordingly, President Richard Nixon decided to enforce a peace agreement by effectively bombing the North Vietnamese back to the negotiating table.

Thus, on 14 December 1972, Nixon handed over control of the military conduct of the Vietnam War to the Chairman of the Joint Chiefs of Staff, Adm Thomas Moorer. His orders were simple and straightforward – Nixon simply told him to 'win this war'.

Moorer determined to do this through the massive application of air power, and ordered a new, full-scale aerial assault on North Vietnam under the codename *Linebacker II*, attacking targets vital to the country's military forces, economy and 'national prestige'. The initial plan scheduled attacks for three days, targeting enemy air bases, missile sites, oil storage facilities, ammunition dumps and railroad networks, and including targets in and around Hanoi and Haiphong.

The first *Linebacker II* raid was launched on 18 December 1972. Col James R McCarthy, head of the 43rd SW on Guam, briefed his crews that morning and started off with the words, 'Gentlemen, your target for tonight is Hanoi'. Everybody knew how well-defended the North Vietnamese capital was, and McCarthy later said that for the rest of the briefing 'you could have heard a pin drop'.

The first raid saw 129 bombers despatched from Andersen and U-Tapao. The 43rd SW sent out 33 B-52Ds, each loaded with 66 M117 bombs, while the co-located 72nd SW (Provisional) despatched 54 B-52Gs, each carrying 27 bombs internally. The 307th BW at U-Tapao contributed 42 B-52Ds to the operation, each carrying 108 750-lb bombs.

The basic route followed by Andersen-based B-52s saw them rendezvous with Okinawa-based tankers north of Luzon. A pre-planned series of dog-leg 'timing triangles' were available to the tankers and the bombers to ensure that they made their planned time. Since it took 17 minutes to top-up the B-52's tanks even in an uninterrupted contact, the refuelling track had to be long enough to allow for losses of contact and multiple hook-ups. The tankers returned directly to Okinawa, passing the southernmost tip of Taiwan. The bombers then flew on to South Vietnam, generally following set routes to their target areas. The B-52s from U-Tapao flew directly to their targets, over-flying neutral Laos or Cambodia (*USAF*)

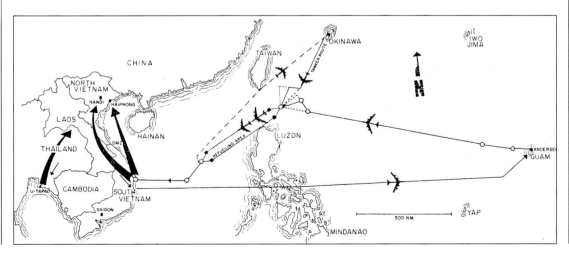

It took one hour and forty-three minutes for the 87 B-52s, led by Maj Bill Stocker, to taxi out and take-off from Andersen. This huge fleet would later be joined by 42 B-52Ds from U-Tapao, the 129 aircraft forming three distinct waves that represented the largest armada of bombers assembled since World War 2.

The bomber force was supported by huge numbers of ancillary aircraft, including EA-3 Skywarriors, EB-66 Destroyers and EA-6 Prowlers to jam the enemy radars and EC-121s to plot SAM firings and radars, and to listen in on enemy controllers. These were backed by dedicated F-105 *Wild Weasels* which attacked enemy SAM sites and their radars, while huge numbers of A-7 Corsair IIs, F-111s and F-4 Phantom IIs were on hand to attack airfields and any fighters which got airborne. Finally, KC-135A Stratotankers stood ready to give fuel to these disparate warplanes.

CM/Sgt James Merrell was a highly experienced gunner who had flown on the first 30-aircraft raid against North Vietnam. He was also in the gun turret of a B-52D for the first *Linebacker II* mission;

'You could tell if a SAM was shot at you not only by your radar returns – you could usually see it out the window! It was exciting, and I wouldn't have given up my seat for anybody because that is what you trained for. You were scared, but you wanted to go.'

The 129 B-52s attacked seven carefully-selected targets. These were the fighter bases at Kep, Hoa Lac and Phuc Yen, the railway yards at Yen Vien, the vehicle repair facility warehouse and storage complex at Kinh No, the Hanoi railroad repair facility and the Hanoi radio station

The B-52s had to run an impressive gauntlet of defensive fire, with more than 200 SAMs being launched against them. They also had to contend with enemy fighters. The first wave hit the airfield at Hoa Lac, a storage area at Kinh No and the railway yards at Yen Vien. Two SAMs were fired at the first cell over Hoa Lac, while the second wave was intercepted by a pair of MiG-21s.

Shortly after coming off target, S/Sgt Samuel O Turner, gunner on board B-52D 56-0676 ('Brown 3'), was warned that a MiG-21 had painted his aircraft with its radar;

'As he closed in on us, I also picked him up on my radar when he was a few miles from our aircraft. A few second later the fighter locked onto us. As the MiG closed in, I also locked onto him. He came in fairly low in a

B-52D-35-BW 56-0676 was the aircraft in which S/Sgt Samuel O Turner downed a VNAF MiG-21 on the first *Linebacker II* raid. Flying as 'Brown 3', the bomber was sent to attack Hoa Lac airfield. The aircraft is seen here flying over the Gulf of Mexico during October 1976 while serving with the 96th BW (*Robert F Dorr*)

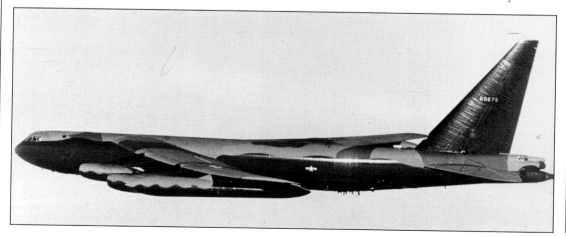

rapid climb. While tracking the first MiG, I picked up a second enemy aircraft at "eight o'clock" at a range of about 7.5 miles. As the attacking MiG came into firing range, I fired a burst. There was a gigantic explosion to the rear of the aircraft. I looked out of the window but was unable to see directly where the MiG-21 would have been. Except for one aeroplane at our "eight o'clock", there was nothing, and within 15 seconds he broke away.'

Another gunner witnessed the flash, and the kill was confirmed, although Vietnamese records fail to show that any fighters were lost on that day.

Gen John C Meyer, SAC's C-in-C (and World War 2 fighter ace), presents S/Sgt Samuel O Turner with the Silver Star in the wake of his successful MiG-21 shoot down on 18 September 1972 (*Robert F Dorr*)

At Kinh No, 'Lilac 03' (B-52D 56-0678) was hit by a SAM 20 seconds before reaching the target. The aircraft was unable to drop its bombs, but it did limp back to U-Tapao. At Yen Vien, B-52G 58-0201 ('Charcoal 1') was shot down after being hit by two SAMs, and another was damaged. 'Charcoal 1' burst into flames and then stalled, falling into a flat spin and crashing to earth like a burning leaf. Eyewitnesses were amazed that three crew escaped from the crippled bomber.

The second wave hit Yen Vien and Kinh No again, and also attacked Gia Lam. B-52G 58-0246 ('Peach 2') was hit by a SAM, but its seven-man crew nursed it back to Thailand, where they baled out successfully.

The third wave attacked Radio Hanoi and the railway repair works at Gia Lam. B-52D 56-0608 ('Rose 1') was shot down by a SAM and B-52D 56-0583 ('Rainbow 1') was also hit, but made it back to U-Tapao. Two MiG-21s appeared but made no contact with the bombers.

More than 200 SAMs had been fired and several MiG-21s sortied. In all, two B-52Gs and a U-Tapao-based B-52D were downed, and two further D-models from Andersen were forced to divert to U-Tapao with serious battle damage. All bar two of the 129 B-52s had reached their targets, although two G-models in the first wave – 'Aqua 2' and 'Red 03' – had problems which prevented them from dropping their bombs.

Day two (19 December) saw the launch of 93 B-52s, 90 of which would bomb successfully. These comprised 33 B-52Ds from the 43rd

The famous MiG-killing B-52D is seen here on the Dyess ramp between sorties. The aircraft subsequently served with the 22nd BW at March AFB and the 92nd BW at Fairchild, before ending its career as the last D-model in service with the 43rd SW at Andersen AFB. The aircraft was then flown out of Andersen by Col Dudley M Moorhous, the 43rd's commander, who had been the first man to reach 300 combat missions in the B-52D. The bomber was preserved at Fairchild AFB following its retirement (*Author's collection*)

This close-up of 56-0676 shows the kill marking applied to the aircraft's nose, as well as the 96th BW's distinctive unit badge (*Author's collection*)

BW, 36 B-52Gs from the 72nd and 24 B-52Ds from the 307th.

The first wave re-visited Kinh No, while the second hit Radio Hanoi and the Bac Giang shipping centre. One B-52G strayed from its place in formation and suffered minor damage when it hit U-Tapao-based B-52D 56-0592 ('Ivory 1'), which had to divert to Nam Phong. The third wave hit Yen Vien and a thermal powerplant at Thai Nguyen. More than 180 SAMs were fired at the B-52s, but none were lost.

An impressive 99 B-52s were launched on Day Three (20 December), with 24 B-52Ds and 30 B-52Gs from Andersen and 45 B-52Ds from U-Tapao. To counter this armada, the North Vietnamese put up their most effective and intense flak barrage yet, launching 220 SAMs against the big bombers and bringing down no fewer than six – four B-52Gs and two B-52Ds, with a third D-model badly damaged.

The first wave on Day Three attacked the Yen Vien railway yards, the railhead at Gia Lam and warehouses at Ai Mo. 'Quilt 3' (B-52G 57-6496) lost two of its ECM jammers and was shot down. Another G-model (57-6481 'Brass 2') was also hit, losing four engines, but the machine successfully limped to Thailand, where the crew baled out. Maj John Stuart's 'Orange 3' (B-52D 56-0622) was less fortunate, going down over the target after being hit by a SAM. Stuart's co-pilot and navigator went 'into the cage', but the rest of the crew were MIA.

The second wave attacked the Thai Nguyen thermal powerplant, Bac Giang and Gia Lam without loss, although two cells of B-52Gs were recalled because of the heavy losses suffered during the first wave attacks.

The third wave was less fortunate, as it attacked Kinh No and Gia Lam. 'Straw 2' (B-52D 56-0669) became the 43rd BW's first *Linebacker* II loss when it was hit as it turned off its IP onto its target run, having lost two ECM jammers. The aircraft was nursed to the Laotian border, where all but the radar navigator abandoned the aircraft safely. The B-52G carrying the Deputy Mission Commander was the next to go down, 'Olive 1' (58-0198) falling in flames over the target. 'Tan 3' (B-52G 58-0169) lost its radar and turned out of the formation, only to be downed moments later a SAM. The tail gunner was the sole survivor. 'Brick 2' (B-52D 55-0067) was also hit, but returned to base. The third wave had lost three out of 21 aircraft, with ten crewmen killed and four taken prisoner.

It could have been much worse, since many SAMs had come perilously close to hitting other B-52s. Some D-model gunners reported seeing SA-2s pass so close that they could make out the cyrillic characters on the side and smell their distinctive exhaust efflux!

'Dan D' flew on the third *Linebacker* raid as a junior co-pilot;

'I'm personally proud of what I did in *Linebacker II*, but I would not talk about it in public. Too many people have contrasting views about Vietnam, and it's still something that can cause unpleasantness and misunderstandings. But between you and I, it was a great success. We lost some good men, but I'm still convinced that we brought the war to an end, and (except on Day Three) the loss rate was far lower than anyone had dared plan for.

'And professionally it was hugely rewarding. We flew more sorties in one night than a typical Stateside base flew in an entire month! We flew with defects which would have forced us to cancel peacetime missions, and the whole ethos went from a deliberate, unhurried, nuclear "Peace is our Profession" approach, to a more urgent, rushed and can-do process. If you had a problem you just had to ask, "Can the aeroplane get over the target, and can it drop its bombs when it gets there?" If the answer was yes, then you went. Some aeroplanes even took off carrying groundcrew who worked on minor repairs as the aircraft flew the long transit to Hanoi – the "Buff" can carry up to ten people, and the normal crew was only six!

'Because it was so tight getting so many aeroplanes airborne in such a short time, we practiced a "roll forward" approach to aborts. If an aircraft in one cell had to abort as it taxied, an aircraft from the cell behind would "roll forward" and replace it, its place being taken in a similar fashion. You'd take over the callsign and mission of the aircraft you replaced. This could lead to some confusion. For example, on one night the aircraft in the cell in front of us reported that he'd been hit by a SAM, using the callsign I'd briefed with! My first reaction was to look across at my co-pilot, wondering if he'd made the call!

'Once over the target, you didn't really take evasive action. On Day One they'd been briefed to fly straight and level on the IP to target run, thus ensuring accuracy and avoiding collateral damage, as well as maintaining the integrity of the three-ship cell, which ensured the effectiveness of the ECM kit. By Day Three, coordinated evasive manoeuvres by the whole cell were permitted, but there was still a real feeling that you should cruise on straight ahead if you possibly could. I don't know why losses were so high on 20 December. Someone said that several of the shot down

On short finals to Marham, in Norfolk, in 1980, B-52D-55-BO 55-0087 boasts the ultimate Phase V ECM antenna array below its rear fuselage. It was this ECM suite which gave the B-52D the edge it enjoyed over the B-52G during *Linebacker II*. This aircraft had deployed to Marham for Exercise *Open Gate*, which saw its crew perform long missions out over the Mediterranean (*Robert F Dorr*)

B-52D 56-0604 takes off from Andersen in late 1972, laden with 500-lb bombs. This aircraft was once named *East to Westover*, reflecting its origin as a 99th BW machine – the wing was, of course, based at Westover AFB, Massachusetts. 56-0604 was retired to the 'boneyard' in late 1978 (*Robert F Dorr*)

aircraft had run into a 100-knot jetstream as they dropped down after their bomb runs, leaving them 100 knots slower, and thus more vulnerable and easier to hit. Others said that some guys were manoeuvring too hard to avoid the SAMs, and in doing so they broke the mutual electronic cover you got in a cell.'

On the fourth day (21/22 December) the USAF began the second phase of *Linebacker II*, maintaining the pressure, but with rather fewer sorties. Some 30 *Linebacker* sorties were scheduled each day, and for the next few days (until Day Eight) these would be flown almost exclusively from U-Tapao, while Andersen's aircraft flew *Arc Lights*. There was particular concern about the B-52G, and especially about those G-models which had not received the Phase V ECM upgrade (about half of the aircraft at Andersen). All four B-52Gs downed on Day Three had been to this more basic standard.

The lightly-built B-52G had proved extremely vulnerable to hostile SAMs, and six would be shot down during *Linebacker*. Only one B-52G was able to survive being damaged by a SAM, while several B-52Ds hit by SA-2s were able to land safely.

There was also concern about some of the aircrew. There was vandalism of the O-Clubs at both Andersen and U-Tapao, sarcastic remarks and disruption during briefings, and a rash of crew members asking to be taken off flight status for 'medical' reasons. Andersen experienced several doubtful 'technical aborts', and one pilot was discharged when he spoke out publicly, urging a change in tactics.

The fourth day's 30 *Linebacker* sorties were flown from U-Tapao only, with Andersen-based aircraft flying *Arc Light* sorties in the south. The 30 aircraft attacked Quang Te airfield, the Bac Mai storage facility and a warehouse complex at Van Dien. Two *Linebacker* jets were downed by SAMs, 'Scarlet 1' (B-52D 55-0061) surviving a MiG intercept only to be hit by an SA-2 near Bac Mai. 'Blue 1' (B-52D 55-0050) was shot down by two SA-2s on its bomb run – the crew survived, but all became PoWs.

The fifth day's *Linebacker* missions against Haiphong's railway yards and POL storage areas (on 22 December) were again all flown by B-52Ds from U-Tapao only, all 30 jets receiving excellent support from *Iron Hand* F-105s that reduced SAM firings to about 65 missiles. There were no losses. Andersen-based aircraft (22 B-52Gs and six B-52Ds) flew *Arc Light* sorties in the south.

Twelve B-52Ds from Andersen and 18 B-52Ds from U-Tapao attacked the Lang Dong railway yards north of Haiphong, as well as three nearby SAM sites (VN537, VN563 and VN660) on Day Six (23 December).

The latter were a great challenge, their proximity to the Chinese border forcing the bombers to attack and withdraw along a very narrow axis. Fortunately, only 40 SAMs were fired and no B-52Ds were damaged. Six Andersen-based B-52Ds and 36 B-52Gs flew *Arc Light* sorties that day, while 22 B-52Ds moved from Guam to U-Tapao to bolster the 307th BW as it bore the brunt of the *Linebacker* offensive.

On Day Seven (24 December) U-Tapao contributed 30 *Linebacker* sorties against the Kep and Thai Nguyen railway yards near Hanoi, while Andersen's bombers flew a further 30 *Arc Lights*. For the third consecutive day, there were no B-52 losses, and only 19 SAMs were fired. One B-52D ('Purple Two') was damaged by AAA, however – the first, and only, time a B-52 was hit by gunfire.

The gunner of 'Ruby Three', A1C Albert E Moore, claimed a MiG-21 kill on Day Seven. Moore picked up a fast moving blip on his radar scope, and, after telling the EWO to drop chaff and flares, locked onto the enemy aircraft at a distance of 4000 yards. He fired at 2000 yards, and Moore and another gunner saw an explosion. His claim was accepted, but three other MiG-21 kill claims were not allowed.

Nixon ordered a cessation of bombing for 24 hours in observance of Christmas and as a gesture of goodwill. The North Vietnamese reaction to this lull was carefully and closely watched, and Nixon found it wanting. *Linebacker II* therefore resumed on Boxing Day.

The campaign entered its third, and final, phase on Day Eight (26 December), the intention being to 'turn the screw' by launching a new wave of 'maximum effort' strikes. US tactics changed on Day Eight, with the launch of a single near-simultaneous mass assault by 120 aircraft against 120 targets in ten main groups, with a common bomb release time. It was hoped that this would entirely over-stretch and saturate the defences. The attacking force comprised 42 B-52Ds from U-Tapao and 33 B-52Ds and 45 B-52Gs from Andersen, the mission being led by Maj Bill Stocker in 56-0680, which also carried the 45th BW's charismatic commander, Col McCarthy – the latter flew even though he was suffering from a severe bout of flu. The B-52Gs were sent against targets which avoided the heaviest concentrations of SAMs around Hanoi.

307th BW B-52D 'Ebony 2' (56-0674) was shot down over Hanoi, and another ('Ash 1' 56-0584) was lost while attempting to make a forced landing at U-Tapao, having taken a SAM hit over the target. Two further

On 24 December A1C Albert Moore shot down a MiG-21 during a *Linebacker II* mission against the Thai Nguyen railway yard while flying in this B-52D-55-BO, 55-0083. The aircraft is now preserved at the USAF academy at Colorado Springs, with a red star kill marking which the aircraft did not wear in service, as well as a post-war bomb log. It is seen here at Andersen AFB in late 1972, resting between sorties (*Robert F Dorr*)

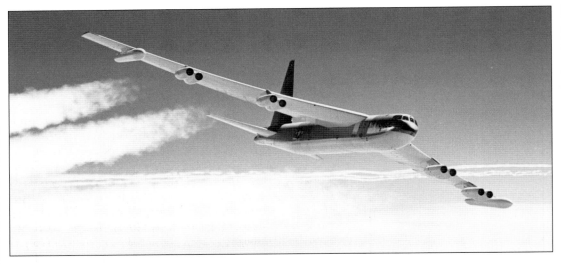

While the B-52F bore the brunt of early bombing operations in Southeast Asia, the B-52Ds continued to fly in the strategic role. Seen in its pre-war colours, B-52D-70-BO 56-0584 went on to fight in Vietnam, where it was eventually lost on 26 December 1972 during *Linebacker II*. Operating as 'Ash 1', the bomber was hit by a SAM over Kinh No but limped back to U-Tapao, where it crashed while attempting to go around. Only the co-pilot and gunner survived (*Author's collection*)

B-52Ds safely returned to Andersen after being damaged by a single SAM which exploded mid-way between them.

The co-pilot of 'Ebony 2', then-1Lt Bob Hudson, remembered the mission clearly, two of the crew (pilot Capt Robert Morris and EWO Capt Nutter Wimbrow) being killed and the rest taken prisoner after abandoning the aircraft. They were lucky to survive;

'One day at a bar a friend of mine, who was an A-6 driver, and who didn't know my background, told me he was slightly behind and below a "Buff" that was going down when it exploded in mid air. He said he had never seen such a violent explosion. I asked him the date, and he said 26 December 1972 – our night!

'The night we got bagged, as we taxied out our gunner got ill. I called for a replacement and I was told I would get one once we reached the hammerhead. At our take-off time a truck pulled up and a guy ran to the back of the aeroplane and climbed in. This guy comes over the intercom and says "I am ready" and we launched. We never got a chance to introduce ourselves, nor to get his name. When we got hit by the second SAM (we were hit by at least three), and after we got the bombs off – all 108 of them, and on target I might add – I gave the order to bale out. The nose of the B-52 pitched violently down, so I assumed our gunner had jumped.

'I found out my gunner's name after I reached Clark and was in the hospital. I am honoured to have flown with Papa Jim Cook, one of the bravest men I have ever met. He had come out with the first group of PoWs due to injuries to his legs. I was able to meet him at Fitzsimmons Army Hospital just after he had had both of his legs amputated.

'Anyway, the wing flew Mike Labeau and my gunner to Germany to be a part of my retirement ceremony, and what a thrill it was to have him there! I finally found out that he had got tangled up in his equipment and rode the aircraft down until a fourth SAM hit the bomber and blew him from the "Buff"!

Bob Hudson never realised that his aircraft had also been claimed as a kill by VNAF ace Pham Tuan of the 921st Sao Dao Fighter Regiment, flying MiG-21MF 'Fishbed-J' 5121, who fired two infrared-homing missiles at the B-52. This was the first of two 'Buff' kills claimed by the

VNAF, 12 of whose pilots had been especially trained to attack the B-52 earlier in the year – eight of them had also received intensive night interception training. Ramming attacks were authorised late in December, although none were carried out. Tuan's aircraft has been preserved in Hanoi at the VNAF Museum in the Dong Da district.

The second aircraft downed on Day Eight was hit by two SAMs over the target. With an engine out, and flames from other engines stretching back past the tail turret, the pilot and co-pilot struggled back to U-Tapao, refuelling three times during the next 90 minutes. Tragically, the crew lost control as they tried to obey an ATC command to over-shoot. The aircraft slammed onto the ground beside the airfield and began to burn.

A pilot who had just returned from his mission, Maj Brent Diefenbach, leapt from his crew bus on the perimeter track, negotiated the base's barbed wire and hurricane fences and commandeered a Thai minibus. He was driven to the wrecked aircraft, where, without thought for his own safety, he crawled through the flames and pulled the unconscious co-pilot to safety. The tail gunner managed to extricate himself, too, but the rest of the crew were killed.

The accident led to a near-mutiny because the base fire engines had been held back at the main gate, MPs refusing to permit them to leave the airfield to attend the crash site. Frayed tempers were further exacerbated when it became known that consideration was being given to issuing Diefenbach with an official reprimand for his disregard of SAC regulations. Fortunately, sanity prevailed. Both aircraft lost that day had been flying in two-ship cells, the third aircraft having aborted. Thereafter, such formations were prohibited, and all cells had to maintain three aircraft.

The ninth day of *Linebacker II* (27 December) was, in some respects, the highlight of the operation, although it involved fewer aircraft than the day before. While U-Tapao contributed 30 B-52Ds, Andersen despatched nine B-52Ds and 21 B-52Gs, hitting rail, supply and SAM site targets. A total of 120 SAMs were launched against the B-52s, and two were lost. Andersen also mounted 54 *Arc Light* sorties.

One B-52D ('Cobalt 1' 56-0605) was hit near the port wheel well and abandoned by four of the crew, the EWO and radar navigator both dying in the aircraft. The aircraft may have been the VNAF's second bomber kill, since Vu Xuan Thieu claimed to have shot down a B-52 in the same area at the same time, although his own aircraft disintegrated as it flew through the debris of 'Cobalt 1'. The USAF has always maintained that 56-0605 was downed by a SAM, and continue to deny that any B-52s were shot down by VNAF fighters.

'Ash 2' (B-52D 56-0599) was hit by an SA-2 ten seconds after bombing a SAM site. All the crew were injured, but Capt John Mize kept the aircraft in the air and limped back to Thai airspace, where they baled out safely.

Lt Col Gerald Wickline flew his first sortie over Hanoi on Day Nine, as he later recalled;

'We flew our first mission over Hanoi on the 27th. Believe me, you can't believe how bad it was. Our target was a railway yard on the north side of Hanoi. We saw well over 100 SAMs fired and more than 30 of them came within one mile of our aeroplane, with at least half of those missing us by less than 200 ft. My mouth was so full of cotton I could barely talk, and the whole time I thought I would be dead the next second. There was no way to outmanoeuvre them, and several times I was blinded by a near-missile detonation, or from the brilliant glare of their rocket trail as they went past me. The B-52 right behind me was shot down, with no survivors listed as of this time.

'The mission over Hanoi on 27 December was a nightmare that I will not soon forget. I found out on that sortie that I was not a coward. I begged for an excuse to turn that aeroplane around and not fly through those missiles, but I was more afraid of being branded a coward than I was of dying.'

On the penultimate day of the operation (Day Ten, 28 December) the effort was concentrated against missile sites and SAM storage facilities, as well as the Lang Dang railway yard and Duc Noi. The 43rd and 72nd SWs each sent 15 aircraft, while 30 B-52Ds were sortied from U-Tapao. None were lost, and only 27 SAMs were fired.

On Day 11 (29 December) things followed a similar pattern. Andersen despatched 18 B-52Ds and 12 B-52Gs, while U-Tapao again sent out 30 aircraft. These bombed the Phuc Yen SAM support facility, the Tra Cam SAM storage area and the Lang Dang railway yards. No B-52s were shot down, but several were engaged. Geoff Engels, a B-52G pilot from Loring AFB, found himself captaining the last aircraft in the last cell of *Linebacker II* ('Gray 3'). The aircraft was hit by fragments from several (probably nine) SAMs, but limped home leaking like a sieve from what were later counted as 117 holes! The aircraft lost its autopilot and HF radio, and some engines were damaged.

A senior officer on the ground directed Engels to take on fuel from an accompanying tanker, but he declined, feeling that he had sufficient fuel to get back. He was also worried that putting fuel into a system which was badly holed might cause further problems, and he did not want to land with anything approaching full tanks. Nor did he want to retract the undercarriage and flaps (necessary to refuel), which had already been extended for a controllability check. The officer tried to give Engels a 'Letter of Admonition' when he landed, but instead the young pilot received a well-deserved DFC. As the last crew to be fired at during *Linebacker*, Engels' men became known as 'the last of the missile magnets'.

Even as the final waves of B-52s were still in the air, Eighth Air Force HQ was directed that all bombing raids above the 20th parallel would cease after the Day 11 jets had landed. Just after noon on 30 December 1972, this event occurred when the last B-52G recovered at Andersen.

On 30 December President Nixon announced that negotiations would resume in Paris on 8 January, and immediately restricted all bombing attacks to targets below the 20th parallel, with the B-52s being tasked to fly just 36 daily *Arc Lights* until further notice. These were not without loss, however, and on 4 January 1973 Lt Col Gerald Wickline became the last B-52 pilot to be shot down in the Vietnam War;

'Our target was a truck park 15 miles northwest of Vinh, which is just below the 20th parallel. We were the next to last aeroplane in a nine-aeroplane wave. Our call sign was "Ruby 2". At about the IP we picked up some SAM signals and started our SAM manoeuvres. We saw lots of AAA fire over Vinh – more that I have ever seen before – including the two missions over Hanoi.

'At about 40 seconds TTG (time to target), four missiles were fired at us, off our left wing. I manoeuvred to avoid No 1 and No 2, with No 1 going past our nose (really close) and detonating just above us (going up). No 2 SAM missed our tail by an estimated 50 ft and also detonated just above us. I had lost sight of Nos 3 and 4, and we were close to TTG zero, so I rolled level, and simultaneously with bombs away, there was a tremendous explosion directly below our nose. Three windows on my side of the aeroplane shattered, showering us with broken bits of glass.

'The No 1 engine fire light came on and a blazing fire was burning in the No 1 pod. All of my flight instruments, including airspeed and altitude, were inoperative. Most of the engine instruments on both sides of the cockpit were inoperative, the glass having been shattered in most of them. All hydraulic power to the left wing was out and all fuel gauges on the left wing were either spinning or stuck.

'I polled the crew and everyone answered but the tail gunner. No one was hurt at this time, but a couple of minutes later the radar navigator (RN) called in a fuel leak that had just developed above his head, and fuel was pouring in right on top of him, and shortly he started screaming from the pain of the fuel burning him – these were chemical burns.

'We got out over the water and turned south, and by this time the RN was screaming from the pain of the JP-4 burns, and the lower deck was literally floating in fuel. We tried continuously to contact the gunner, but to no avail. We started a descent. Soon after level off, we felt a thump and heard a parachute beeper go off. Our gunner had bailed out all on his own as flames from a fire in the belly began licking around his turret.

'The aeroplane was barely controllable. Every time we would attempt to slow down it would start a roll to the right and we could only straighten it out by gaining airspeed. By this time we were abeam Da Nang, so I turned eastbound (away from land) and ordered the bale out. We were almost sure that when the first ejection seat fired we would become a fireball, but thank God that didn't happen. I heard two thumps which I assumed was the navigator and RN ejection seats firing, followed a few seconds later by a third, which was the EWO. I told the co-pilot to go and he squeezed the trigger. I was temporarily blinded by flying debris.

'After I got my eyes cleared and looked, he was gone. I made a call on interphone to see if anyone was still on board, waited a few seconds, then pulled the throttles to idle, assumed the position and squeezed the trigger.

By the end of the war, B-52D-60-BO 55-0101 (also seen on page 53) had been repainted, and looked very much smarter than it had done when photographed just months earlier (*Robert F Dorr*)

I felt a tremendous kick in the seat of my pants, a great blast of cold air, severe tumbling, an extremely sharp jolt tearing the ejection seat from my hands and a loud pop, followed by the most intense silence I have ever heard.

'I could hardly believe my good fortune when I looked up and saw that beautiful big orange and white canopy of the parachute above my head. About that time I felt extremely nauseous, so I pulled my oxygen mask from my face and barfed into the Gulf of Tonkin. I saw a fireball on the horizon. Our B-52 had hit the water and exploded.'

All six of the crew survived their ejections, and all were successfully recovered from the sea.

Linebacker II, popularly known as the 'Eleven Day War', had comprised 3000 sorties, and had seen the expenditure of more than 40,000 tons of bombs in what was the most concentrated air operation of the entire conflict. The B-52 had played a vital role in this campaign, dropping 15,000 tons of bombs in 729 sorties. Two B-52 gunners were officially credited with downing enemy fighters, while hundreds of military targets on the ground were destroyed. On the operation's busiest day, 26 December 1972, 120 B-52s hit several targets during the space of just 15 minutes.

On the debit side 26 aircraft, including 15 B-52 bombers, were lost during the operation, and 31 of the B-52 crewmembers shot down were captured and held as PoWs. A further 93 were listed as Missing In Action at the end of the 11-day operation, although this figure was subsequently reduced to 33 killed or MIA. Interestingly, some 24 B-52s had been hit by enemy SAMs (884 of which were reportedly fired!), but nine (eight of them B-52Ds) had limped back to base.

North Vietnamese sources variously claimed that 1318, 1400 or 1600 civilians had been killed, and that schools, hospitals and even orphanages had been bombed. *Linebacker II* also destroyed 1600 military structures and 372 pieces of railway rolling stock, severely disrupted North Vietnam's rail network, destroyed 25 per cent of the country's POL reserves and removed 80 per cent of electrical generating capacity.

Even in the face of such losses, there was some honour and chivalry on both sides. The body of Col Keith R Heggen, shot down in a B-52, was repatriated in 1974 and he was reburied at the Arlington National Cemetery. Accompanying his body was a hand-carved stone marker that had been placed over his original grave by his North Vietnamese captors When his widow received the stone, the first thing she noticed was that someone had taken the time and trouble to decorate it with a small flower motif.

The stalled peace talks resumed, as Nixon had promised, on 8 January 1973, and exactly one week later the president announced an end to all bombing, mining and shelling of the North Vietnam. A final agreement was reached within 30 days of the final bomb being dropped, with Le Duc Tho and Henry Kissinger formally signing the Paris Peace Accords on 27 January 1973. Within 60 days some 591 American PoWs had been released and returned to the USA, a commission had been appointed to oversee the truce (and any resultant territorial disputes) and North Vietnam had acknowledged the right of the Vietnamese people to determine their own future.

AN UNEASY PEACE

With the signature of the Paris Peace Accords on 27 January 1973, the Vietnam War was over, and the neutrality of Laos and Cambodia had been formally affirmed. On 27 January a 'Buff' (commanded by Capt Donald Becker on his 200th operational B-52 mission) flew the final *Arc Light* mission over South Vietnam, although sorties against targets in Laos and Cambodia continued.

In Laos, the first post-war *Arc Light* was flown on 6 February at the request of the Royal Laotian Government as its forces struggled to regain control of strategic towns and villages from the Pathet Lao. As a direct result of the *Arc Light* sorties, the Pathet Lao agreed to a negotiated cease-fire on 22 February, although B-52 operations continued 24 hours later as a result of widespread cease-fire violations.

The B-52 rejoined the battle against the Khmer Rouge some 72 hours later when President Lon Noi requested USAF air support to attempt to stem the enemy advance. The B-52s remained active over Cambodia until 15 August, flying intensive sorties against enemy training camps, logistics facilities and staging areas as part of Operations *Freedom Deal* and *Scoot*. By the end of March, the Cambodian forces were beginning to make some progress against the insurgents, although pressure on the capital, Phnom Penh, remained intense.

On 12 June, President Nixon announced that all offensive US air operations in Southeast Asia would end on 15 August. The 43rd SW's B-52Ds flew their final 16 *Arc Light* sorties on 11 August, while the 72nd SW's B-52Gs completed their last nine *Arc Light* sorties four days later – the last mission was flown by Capt Vic Putz. Congress

Due to the commitment of large numbers of B-52Ds to the war in Vietnam, and the more rapid-than-predicted consumption of fatigue life, a number of B-52E/Fs enjoyed an extended lease of life. Indeed, some of these aircraft gained SAC's new SIOP camouflage and Hound Dog missiles. The B-52E was finally retired in March 1970, while the B-52F soldiered on until 1978. This aircraft (56-0701) was a B-52E-45-BW (*Philip Jarrett*)

formally ordered the end of US air operations in Southeast Asia later that day. B-52 operations had lasted just over eight years, and 2.63 million tons of bombs had been dropped during 126,615 sorties, for the loss of 31 aircraft. Of the 126,615 sorties, 125,479 reached their targets and 124,532 released their bombs. Some 55 per cent of targets were in South Vietnam, six per cent in the north, 27 per cent in Laos and 12 per cent in Cambodia.

The B-52 force began redeploying to CONUS-based units from 27 September 1973, when the first two B-52Ds from Andersen returned to Carswell AFB. Aircraft continued to return home (to Carswell, Dyess and March) throughout September, while the movement of B-52Gs (initially to Blytheville AFB, Arkansas) began on 30 September. All 71 of the B-52Gs had re-deployed to Barksdale, Fairchild, Mather and Robins by 28 October.

This left some 25 B-52Ds at Andersen, and about twice that number at U-Tapao – the 307th SW at the latter base was finally deactivated on 30 September, being replaced by a rotational deployment from Andersen. The strength at Andersen had declined to a planned 16 aircraft by the end of 1974, with the 43rd SW remaining in-theatre as part of SAC's strategic force, although it continued to fly occasional simulated *Arc Lights* under the code-name *Busy Bubble*.

With the American presence reduced to relatively small numbers of advisers and specialists, North Vietnam invaded South Vietnam again in the spring of 1975, and this time the NVA quickly overran the country.

Thanks to *Linebacker*, the USA had been able to withdraw its troops and equipment 'with honour', and the PoWs had been brought home. Nixon was no longer in office to witness the humiliation as the last US personnel were evacuated as the enemy tanks rolled into Saigon, having been forced to resign over the Watergate scandal the previous August.

The EVS and Phase VI ECM equipped-B-52G was a very much more capable and survivable aircraft than the earlier G-models which had proved so disappointingly vulnerable during *Linebacker II*. Here, a 416th BW B-52G gets airborne from Griffiss AFB, New York, in the mid 1970s (*Author's collection*)

The B-52Ds almost returned to combat in May 1975 following the Khmer Rouge's seizure of the US merchant ship SS *Mayaguez* in international waters off Cambodia. On 13 May 1975, the 43rd Munitions Maintenance Squadron even began loading B-52Ds with bombs, ready to support a recovery mission, although this was cancelled at the last moment.

Following the murder of two US Army officers in the Korean DMZ on 19 August, B-52Ds from Andersen flew daily 'show of force' missions in three-ship cells for the next five days, and thereafter the 43rd SW began training for conventional bombing missions over Korea.

But the B-52 force remained active outside Southeast Asia, too. The 1973 Arab-Israeli War led to an immediate change in SAC's alert status, and plans for a deployment of aircraft to the Middle East were put in train. But the primary arena for the 'Buff' remained the Cold War, and as the conflict in Vietnam drew to a close, SAC's fleet of Stratofortresses continued to stand alert duties, while developing new doctrine, tactics and weapons to allow it to remain viable into the coming decades.

After their brief action in Vietnam, the B-52Fs reverted to strategic duties, some being modified as Hound Dog missile carriers, and even receiving the so-called Single Integrated Operational Plan (SIOP) camouflage. They enjoyed a long and productive career with SAC's Cold War deterrent force, and the last B-52F (57-0171) in service was finally retired from the 2nd BW at Barksdale on 7 December 1978.

Once expected to retire in 1971, the B-52D lasted even longer. After its participation in the Vietnam War, the D-models was modified to extend their service lives and to give improved capabilities. Many individual aircraft had amassed more than double their planned 5000-

Apart from a couple of aircraft deployed to launch D-21 reconnaissance drones, the 'top-of-the-line' B-52H played no part in the war in Southeast Asia, being retained in CONUS for nuclear deterrent duties. Aircrew from B-52H units did take their turn in helping man the deployed units, however. B-52H-140-BW 60-0017 is seen in typical late 1960s configuration, painted in SIOP camouflage, but with no EVS turrets and the original short tailcone (*Philip Jarrett*)

hour lives, but a core fleet of 80 aircraft were extensively rebuilt. Although they retained their tactical-looking, Vietnam-era camouflage, the D-models returned to the strategic role, and some even gained Hound Dog capability. The aircraft did retain a vital conventional capability, however, and from 1977 some B-52Ds were modified to carry GBU-15 glide bombs, under a $5 million programme. The modified B-52Ds could carry two GBU-15s in tandem under each wing, or one GBU-15 and the necessary datalink pod.

The last operational D-model mission was finally flown by the 20th BMS at Carswell on 1 October 1983.

But while the Vietnam War stalwart D- and F-models saw useful post-war use, the backbone of SAC during the mid- and late-1970s was provided by the B-52G/H. From 15 October 1971, about 270 B-52G/Hs were armed with a new stand-off weapon, the Boeing AGM-69A short-range attack missile (SRAM). This was to be carried in place of the ageing 'Hound Dog', although its relatively small size and low weight allowed aircraft to sortie a much larger number of missiles – up to 20 in total, with 12 carried externally on the underwing pylons and eight more on a rotary launcher in the rear section of the bomb-bay. The first B-52Gs with SRAM re-entered service with the 42nd BW in March 1972.

During the 1970s, the B-52G/Hs were also equipped with new sensors to enhance their all-weather capability. Between 1972 and 1976, both models were fitted with the AN/ASQ-151 Electro-optical Viewing System (EVS), consisting of a turret-mounted Westinghouse AN/AVQ-22 Low-Light-Level Television (LLTV) camera housed under the port forward fuselage and a Hughes AN/AAQ-6 forward-looking infrared (FLIR) sensor to starboard. To enhance the big bomber's survivability, the newer short-tailed B-52s also gained a Phase VI ECM Defensive Avionics Systems (ECP2519) upgrade as part of the *Rivet Ace* programme.

B-52G-100-BW 58-0204 was used as the *Rivet Ace* testbed, fitted with the advanced Phase VI ECM system which redressed the shortcomings revealed over Vietnam. The aircraft has a test-fit of an AN/ALQ-153 emitter in a fairing on the port tailplane tip, and carries a load of SRAM missiles. The aircraft went on to participate in the Cruise missile fly off (between the AGM-86 and AGM-109), before returning to frontline service. 58-0204 flew six missions in *Desert Storm* as *Special Delivery*, operating from RAF Fairford and Moron, in Spain. (*Author's collection*)

With the B-52D continuing primarily in the tactical and conventional roles, the B-52G/H formed the backbone of the USAF's strategic nuclear deterrent.

The steady improvement of Soviet nuclear weapons, and the abandonment of airborne alert, saw a greater emphasis placed on rapid

B-52G/Hs began to receive EVS turrets in 1971, and the programme was completed in 1976. EVS-equipped aircraft were not deployed to Southeast Asia, however (*Robert F Dorr*)

The 449th BW flew B-52Hs from Kincheloe AFB, Michigan, from 1963 until 1977. This B-52H (60-0013) remains in service today, and was one of the first of the breed to adopt a conventional role, equipped with AGM-84 Harpoon anti-ship missiles (*Philip Jarrett*)

reaction take offs by nuclear-armed bombers. Under the $35 million project *Quick Start*, launched in 1974, cartridge starters were fitted to all unmodified B-52G/H engines (aircraft had received such starters on two engines in 1963-64), allowing much more rapid 'scramble' take-offs and dramatically improving reaction times.

Finally, cruise missiles were added during the 1980s, and the aircraft's employment with these revolutionary weapons will be chronicled in a later volume.

APPENDICES

APPENDIX A:

B-52 PRODUCTION AND SERIAL BLOCKS

Block	Serials	Quantity	Cumulative Total	Block	Serials	Quantity	Cumulative Total
XB-52-BO	49-0230	1	1	B-52E-45-BW	56-0699 to -0712	14	300
YB-52-BO	49-0231	1	2	B-52E-90-BO	57-0014 to -0022	9	309
B-52A-1-BO	52-001 to -003	3	5	B-52E-95-BO	57-0023 to -0029	7	316
RB-52B-5-BO	52-004 to -006	3	8	B-52F-100-BO	57-0030 to -0037	8	324
RB-52B-10-BO	52-007 to -0013	7	15	B-52F-105-BO	57-0038 to -0052	15	339
RB-52B-15-BO	52-8710 to -8715	6	21	B-52F-110-BO	57-0053 to -0073	21	360
RB-52B-20-BO	52-8716	1	22	B-52E-50-BW	57-0095 to -0109	15	375
RB-52B-25-BO	53-0366 to -0372	7	29	B-52E-55-BW	57-0110 to -0130	21	396
B-52B-25-BO	53-0373 to -0376	4	33	B-52E-60-BW	57-0131 to -0138	8	404
RB-52B-30-BO	53-0377 to -0379	3	36	B-52F-65-BW	57-0139 to -0154	16	420
B-52B-30-BO	53-0380 to -0387	8	44	B-52F-70-BW	57-0155 to -0183	29	449
B-52B-35-BO	53-0388 to -0398	11	55	B-52G-75-BW	57-6468 to -6475	8	457
B-52C-40-BO	53-0399 to -0408	10	65	B-52G-80-BW	57-6476 to -6485	10	467
B-52C-45-BO	54-2664 to -2675	12	77	B-52G-85-BW	57-6486 to -6499	14	481
B-52C-50-BO	54-2676 to -2688	13	90	B-52G-90-BW	57-6500 to -6520	21	502
B-52D-1-BW	55-0049 to -0051	3	93	B-52G-95-BW	58-0158 to -0187	30	532
B-52D-5-BW	55-0052 to -0054	3	96	B-52G-100-BW	58-0188 to -0211	24	556
B-52D-10-BW	55-0055 to -0060	6	102	B-52G-105-BW	58-0212 to -0232	21	577
B-52D-15-BW	55-0061 to -0064	4	106	B-52G-110-BW	58-0233 to -0246	14	591
B-52D-20-BW	55-0065 to -0067	3	109	B-52G-115-BW	58-0247 to -0258	12	603
B-52D-20-BW	55-0673 to -0675	3	112	B-52G-120-BW	59-2564 to -2575	12	615
B-52D-25-BW	55-0676 to -0680	5	117	B-52G-125-BW	59-2576 to -2587	12	627
B-52D-55-BO	55-0068 to -0088	21	138	B-52G-130-BW	59-2588 to -2602	15	642
B-52D-60-BO	55-0089 to -0104	16	154	B-52H-135-BW	60-0001 to -0013	13	655
B-52D-65-BO	55-0105 to -0117	13	167	B-52H-140-BW	60-0014 to -0021	8	663
B-52D-70-BO	56-0580 to -0590	11	178	B-52H-145-BW	60-0022 to -0033	12	675
B-52D-75-BO	56-0591 to -0610	20	198	B-52H-150-BW	60-0034 to -0045	12	687
B-52D-80-BO	56-0611 to -0630	20	218	B-52H-155-BW	60-0046 to -0057	12	699
B-52E-85-BO	56-0631 to -0649	19	237	B-52H-160-BW	60-0058 to -0062	5	704
B-52E-90-BO	56-0650 to -0656	7	244	B-52H-165-BW	61-0001 to -0013	13	717
B-52D-30-BW	56-0657 to -0668	12	256	B-52H-170-BW	61-0014 to -0026	13	730
B-52D-35-BW	56-0669 to -0680	12	268	B-52H-175-BW	61-0027 to -0040	14	744
B-52D-40-BW	56-0681 to -0698	18	286				

APPENDIX B

VIETNAM B-52 LOSSES

Date	Type and Serial	Operator	Aircraft/ Crew	Callsign	Notes
18 June 1965	B-52F 57-0047	3960th BW	320th BW	-	mid-air collision before first AAR, 8 killed, 4 survived on both aircraft
18 June 1965	B-52F 57-0179	3960th BW	7th BW	-	mid-air collision before first AAR
7 July 1967	B-52 56-0595	4133rd BW	22nd BW	-	mid-air collision near IP, 6 killed, 7 survived on both aircraft
7 July 1967	B-52 56-0627	4133rd BW	454th BW	-	mid-air collision near IP
8 July 1967	B-52 56-0601	4133rd BW	22nd BW	-	crashed during attempted forced landing at Da Nang
18 November 1968	B-52 55-0103	4252nd SW	306th BW	-	burned after aborted take-off from Kadena
3 December 1968	B-52 55-0115	4252nd SW	306th BW	-	destroyed by ground fire at Kadena
10 May 1969	B-52 56-0593	4133rd BW	509th BW	-	crashed into sea after take-off from Andersen
19 July 1969	B-52 56-0676	307th SW	70th BW	-	burned after aborted take-off from U-Tapao
27 July 1969	B-52 56-0630	-	70th BW	-	structural failure after take-off from Andersen, 8 killed
8 July 1972	B-52G 59-2600	72nd SW	70th BW	-	lost ASI on take-off from Andersen and crashed into sea, 1 killed, 5 survived
30 July 1972	B-52 56-0677	307th SW	?/? BW		hit by lightning over Thailand, lost control
15 October 1972	B-52 55-0097	307th SW	-	-	damaged on landing, scrapped February 1973
22 November 1972	B-52 55-0110	307th SW	?/96th BW	'Olive 2'	hit by SA-2 over Vinh, crew baled out near Thai border
18/19 December 1972	B-52G 58-0201	72nd SW	?/97th BW	'Charcoal 1'	hit by SA-2 and crashed at Yen Vien, 3 killed, 3 PoW
18/19 December 1972	B-52G 58-0246	72nd SW	?/2nd BW	'Peach 2'	hit by SA-2 near Kinh No, crew baled out over Thailand
18/19 December 1972	B-52D 56-0608	-	99th/? BW	'Rose 1'	hit by SA-2 and crashed near Hanoi, 4 PoW, 2 MIA
20/21 December 1972	B-52G 57-6496	72nd SW	?/456th BW	'Quilt 3'	hit by SA-2 and crashed near Yen Vien, 2 killed, 4 PoW
20/21 December 1972	B-52G 57-6481	72nd SW	?/42nd BW	'Brass 2'	hit by SA-2 near Yen Vien, crew baled out over Thailand
20/21 December 1972	B-52D 56-0622	307th SW	7th/99th BW	'Orange 3'	hit by SA-2 and crashed near Yen Vien, 2 PoW, 4 MIA
20/21 December 1972	B-52D 56-0669	43rd SW	306th/? BW	'Straw 2'	hit by SA-2 over Hanoi, crew baled out over Laos, 1 killed
20/21 December 1972	B-52G 58-0198	72nd SW	?/92nd BW	'Olive 1'	hit by SA-2 and crashed near Kinh No, 4 killed, 3 PoW
20/21 December 1972	B-52G 58-0169	72nd SW	?/97th BW	'Tan 3'	hit by SA-2 and crashed near Kinh No, 5 killed, 1 PoW
22/23 December 1972	B-52D 55-0061	307th SW	96th/22nd BW	'Scarlet 1'	survived MiG intercept then hit by SA-2 near Bac Mai, 1 killed, 2 MIA, 3 PoW
22/23 December 1972	B-52D 55-0050	307th SW	43rd/7th BW	'Blue 1'	hit by two SA-2s, crew PoW
26/27 December 1972	B-52D 56-0674	307th SW	96th/449rd BW	'Ebony 2'	hit by SA-2, 2 killed, 4 PoW. Claimed as kill by MiG-21 pilot
26/27 December 1972	B-52D 56-0584	307th SW	22nd/? BW	'Ash 1'	hit by SA-2 near Kinh No, crashed on landing at U-Tapao, 4 killed, 2 survived
27/28 December 1972	B-52D 56-0599	307th SW	7th/28th BW	'Ash 2'	hit by SA-2 near Hanoi, crew bailed out over Laos
27/28 December 1972	B-52D 56-0605	43rd SW	7th/320th BW	'Cobalt 1'	hit by SA-2 near Trung Quan and crashed, 2 killed, 4 PoW. Claimed as kill by MiG-21 pilot
4 January 1973	B-52D 55-0056	307th SW	-	-	hit by SA-2 over Vinh, crew baled out 'feet wet'
13 January 1973	B-52D 55-0116	307th SW	-	-	force-landed at Da Nang after SA-2 hit. Scrapped 28-29/3/72

Notes

This table lists 17 B-52s lost in combat to enemy action, with two more being scrapped after sustaining battle damage and a further eleven lost in accidents. Interestingly, some USAF documents suggest that 30 B-52s were lost in Vietnam to all causes. The USAF has never admitted that any of the B-52s lost in Vietnam were shot down by enemy fighters, but the VNAF claimed two B-52 kills. Pham Tuan, flying MiG-21 '921', claimed to have shot down a B-52 near Hoa Binh on 27 December, while Vu Xuan Thieu (flying the same MiG-21 the following night) claimed to have downed another near Son La. This time the MiG-21 was badly damaged by debris from the B-52. In respect to column four of this table, up until 1970, it may be assumed that aircraft were being flown by crews from the same unit. Thereafter, the unit to whom the aircraft belonged is given first, followed by the crew's parent unit, separated by a slash.

APPENDICES

CREW FATES FROM LOST AIRCRAFT

Date	Aircraft	Callsign	Unit	Crewmember	Position	Status
18/12/72	B-52G 58-0201	'Charcoal 1'	72nd BW(P)	Lt Col Donald Rissi	Pilot	killed in action
				1Lt Robert Thomas	Co-Pilot	killed in action
				Maj Richard Johnson	Radar Navigator	PoW, returned
				Capt Robert Certain	Navigator	PoW, returned
				Capt Richard Simpson	EWO	PoW, returned
				E7 Walter Ferguson	Gunner	killed in action
19/12/72	B-52D 56-0608	'Rose 1'	307th SW	Capt Hal Wilson	Pilot	PoW, returned
				Capt Charles Brown	Co-Pilot	PoW, returned
				Maj Fernando Alexander	Radar Navigator	PoW, returned
				Capt Richard Cooper	Navigator	MIA
				Capt Henry Barrows	EWO	PoW, returned
				E6 Charlie Poole	Gunner	MIA
20/12/72	B-52D 56-0622	'Orange 3'	307th SW	Maj John Stuart	Pilot	MIA
				1Lt Paul Granger	Co-Pilot	PoW, returned
				Maj Randolph Perry	Radar Navigator	MIA
				Capt Thomas Klomann	Navigator	PoW, returned
				Capt Irwin Lerner	EWO	MIA
				E7 Arthur McLaughlin	Gunner	MIA
20/12/72	B-52G 57-6496	'Quilt 3'	72nd BW(P)	Capt Terry Geloneck	Pilot	PoW, returned
				1Lt William Arcuri	Co-Pilot	PoW, returned
				Capt Warren Spencer	Radar Navigator	killed in action
				1Lt Michael Martini	Navigator	PoW, returned
				Capt Craig Paul	EWO	killed in action
				E5 Roy Madden	Gunner	PoW, returned
21/12/72	B-52G 58-0198	'Olive 1'	72nd BW(P)	Lt Col Keith Heggen	Deputy Mission CO	PoW, died in captivity
				Lt Col James Nagahiro	Pilot	PoW, returned
				Capt Donovan Walters	Co-Pilot	killed in action
				Maj Edward Johnson	Radar Navigator	killed in action
				Capt Lynn Beens	Navigator	PoW, returned
				Capt Robert Lynn	EWO	killed in action
				E3 Charles Bebus	Gunner	killed in action
21/12/72	B-52G 58-0169	'Tan 3'	72nd BW(P)	Capt Randall Craddock	Pilot	killed in action
				Capt George Lockhart	Co-Pilot	killed in action
				Maj Bobby Kirby	Radar Navigator	killed in action
				1Lt Charles Darr	Navigator	killed in action
				Capt Ronald Perry	EWO	killed in action
				E5 James Lollar	Gunner	PoW, returned
22/12/72	B-52D 55-0050	'Blue 1'	307th SW	Lt Col John Yuill	Pilot	PoW, returned
				Capt Dave Drummond	Co-Pilot	PoW, returned
				LtCol Lou Bernasconi	Radar Navigator	PoW, returned
				1Lt William Mayall	Navigator	PoW, returned
				Lt Col William Conlee	EWO	PoW, returned
				E5 Gary Morgan	Gunner	PoW, returned
22/12/72	B-52D 55-0061	'Scarlet 3/1'	307th SW	Capt Peter Giroux	Pilot	PoW, returned
				Capt Thomas Bennett	Co-Pilot	MIA
				Lt Col Gerald Alley	Radar Navigator	killed in action
				1Lt Joseph Copack	Navigator	killed in action
				Capt Peter Camerota	EWO	PoW, returned
				E7 Louis LeBlanc	Gunner	PoW, returned

Date	Aircraft	Callsign	Unit	Crewmember	Position	Status
6/12/72	B-52D 56-0674	'Ebony 2'	307th SW	Capt Robert Morris	Pilot	killed in action
				1Lt Robert Hudson	Co-Pilot	PoW, returned
				Capt Michael LaBeau	Radar Navigator	PoW, returned
				1Lt Duane Vavroch	Navigator	PoW, returned
				Capt Nutter Wimbrow	EWO	killed in action
				E6 James Cook	Gunner	PoW, returned
28/12/72	B-52D 56-0605	'Cobalt 2/1'	43rd SW	Capt Frank Lewis	Pilot	PoW, returned
				Capt Samuel Cusimano	Co-Pilot	PoW, returned
				Maj James Condon	Radar Navigator	PoW, returned
				1Lt Bennie Frye	Navigator	killed in action
				Maj Allen Johnson	EWO	killed in action
				E7 James Gough	Gunner	PoW, returned

Notes

This table gives the fates of those aircrew shot down over North Vietnam. Other aircraft were abandoned by their crews after reaching friendly territory, and in most cases survived the ordeal relatively unscathed. Exceptions were the loss of B-52D 56-0669 of the 43rd SW on 20/21 December 1972. 'Straw 2' was hit by an SA-2 over Hanoi, and although the crew baled out safely over Laos, Radio Navigator Maj Frank Gould was lost. The other exception was B-52D 56-0584, which limped back to U-Tapao after being hit by a SAM. The aircraft, with all four engines out on one side, crashed while attempting a go-around. Only co-pilot 1Lt Bob Hymel and gunner T/Sgt Spencer Grippen escaped the ensuing blaze, the remaining four crewmen being killed. Of the 92 crewmembers on board the 15 B-52s lost to enemy action, 26 were recovered, 33 were killed or listed MIA and 33 became PoWs.

APPENDIX D

LINEBACKER II SORTIES AND LOSSES

Day	Date	43rd SW	72nd SW	307th SW	Total
Day 1	18 December 1972	33	54 (2)	42 (1)	129 (3)
Day 2	19 December 1972	33	36	24	93
Day 3	20 December 1972	24 (1)	30 (4)	45 (1)	99 (6)
Day 4	21 December 1972	-	-	30 (2)	30 (2)
Day 5	22 December 1972	-	-	30	30
Day 6	23 December 1972	12	-	18	30
Day 7	24 December 1972	-	-	30	30
Day 8	26 December 1972	33	45	42 (2)	120 (2)
Day 9	27 December 1972	9 (1)	21	30 (1)	60 (2)
Day 10	28 December 1972	15	15	30	60
Day 11	29 December 1972	18	12	30	60
Total		**177 (2)**	**213 (6)**	**351 (7)**	**741 (15)**

Notes

– aircraft losses are in brackets

– the official tally of 724 *Linebacker II* sorties excludes those which turned back, DNCO or which failed to complete due to enemy action

APPENDIX E

B-52 UNITS IN SOUTHEAST ASIA

While in-theatre, B-52s and their crews came under the control of a number of provisional wings, based at Andersen AFB, Guam, U-Tapao RTAB, Thailand, and Kadena AFB, Okinawa. These were re-designated on a number of occasions.

B-52F units contributing aircraft and crews to these wings comprised the 2nd BW at Barksdale AFB, Louisiana, the 7th BW from Carswell AFB, Texas, the 320th BW from Mather AFB, California, and the 454th BW from Colombus AFB, Ohio.

Eleven B-52D wings served 'en masse' in Vietnam. These were the 22nd BW from March AFB, California, the 28th BW from Ellsworth AFB, South Dakota, the 91st BW from Glasgow AFB, Montana, the 92nd SAW from Fairchild AFB, Washington, the 96th SAW from Dyess AFB, Texas, the 99th BW from Westover AFB, Massachusetts, the 306th BW from McCoy AFB, Florida, the 454th BW from Colombus AFB, Ohio, the 461st BW from Amarillo AFB, Texas, the 484th BW from Turner AFB, Georgia, and the 509th BW from Pease AFB, New Hampshire.

Other units, including those equipped with later versions of the B-52, also sent aircrew that had been hastily converted onto the D-model to Southeast Asia. Towards the end of the conflict, B-52Gs were also committed to the campaign.

43rd Strategic Wing

The 43rd SW activated on 1 April 1970, replacing the 3960th SW. The unit was initially responsible for base 'housekeeping' and operations support only, and its only aircraft consisted of five C-97 Stratofreighters. The new wing also took over the responsibilities of the inactivating 4133rd BW (Provisional) on 1 July 1970, and thereafter assumed that wing's Arc Light duties. At that time, the wing controlled a cadre of B-52Ds, and their crews, on six-month TDY from the 96th SAW at Dyess AFB, Texas, with RTU crews assigned for six months from other CONUS-based SAC B-52 units. The 43rd SW included the SAC Contingency Aircrew Training School, through which all new B-52 aircrew in theatre (including those destined for Kadena and U-Tapao) had to pass.

On 16 August 1970, Andersen flew its last Arc Light sorties, and the 43rd SW became part of SAC's nuclear alert force, using alert crews on TDY from U-Tapao. The crews deployed to Andersen for six days alert duty, before rotating home. The wing gained its own B-52s (15 from Ellsworth), and these were given a squadron identity when the 60th BS (Heavy) moved (on paper) from Ramey AFB, Puerto Rico, upon the disbandment of its parent 72nd BW on 30 June 1971. The aircraft were immediately attached to the 307th SW at U-Tapao for Arc Light duties.

The 43rd SW finally gained based B-52s with the first phases of Operation Bullet Shot, as noted in the following listing;

Bullet Shot I – 29 B-52Ds from 7th BW, Carswell AFB, 96th SAW, Dyess AFB, 306th BW, McCoy AFB. 7 February 1972
Bullet Shot II – 22 B-52Ds from 22nd BW, March AFB, 99th BW, Westover AFB, 4 April 1972
Bullet Shot IIA – 6 B-52Ds from 22nd BW, March AFB, 99th BW, Westover AFB, 8 April 1972
Bullet Shot III – 28 B-52Gs from 2nd BW, Barksdale AFB, 11 April 1972
Bullet Shot IV – 5 B-52Gs, 6 May 1972, 7 B-52Gs, 21 May 1972
Bullet Shot V – 58 B-52Gs, 23 May 1972

The B-52Gs were 'hived off' to form the 72nd SW (P) on 1 June 1972, while the 43rd retained responsibility for the D-models, the SCAT School (which returned from U-Tapao) and for host support for the 72nd SW (P). It also gained a second squadron – the 60th BS (P) – to manage the expanded force of B-52Ds.

The 43rd was a co-recipient of the prestigious Collier Trophy in April 1973, awarded for the part it had played in Linebacker II.

On 15 August 1973, the 43rd SW was reassigned to the nuclear deterrent role, and began preparing to return TDY personnel and aircraft to CONUS. It also continued to manage a TDY alert force at U-Tapao, in addition to about 25 of its own aircraft, finally reaching its planned peacetime strength of 16 B-52s during 1975. The wing retired its last B-52D in October 1983, but continued to fly B-52Gs until 1990.

72nd Strategic Wing (Provisional)

With the massive influx of aircraft during Bullet Shot, the B-52D fleet at Andersen AFB rapidly became too large and too unwieldy to be controlled by a single wing. Accordingly, the B-52Gs were 'hived off' to form the 72nd SW (P) on 1 June 1972. The new wing controlled four separate squadrons, namely the 64th, 65th, 329th and the 486th BS (P)s. The wing was inactivated on 15 November 1973, although it had actually shrunk in size once Linebacker II had come to an end.

307th Strategic Wing

The 307th SW at U-Tapao AB, Thailand, activated on 1 April 1970 and took control of all U-Tapao-based B-52Ds from the 4258th SW. The 307th assumed sole responsibility for Arc Light from September 1970 until activity increased again in 1972. It finally inactivated on 30 September 1975. Operational control of the much-reduced B-52 force at U-Tapao had passed to the 364th BS (P) immediately after Linebacker II ended, the unit overseeing all D-model operations from the base until 30 June 1975. It shared this role with the 365th BS (Provisional) until 17 July 1974.

376th Strategic Wing

The 376th SW replaced the 4252nd SW at Kadena AB, Okinawa, on 1 April 1970, and exercised direct control of B-52 Arc Light missions flown from Okinawa until these were terminated in September 1970.

3960th Strategic Wing

The 3960th SW was activated on 1 April 1955, and took responsibility for the TDY B-52 units rotated through Andersen AFB, Guam. This responsibility was passed to the 4133rd BW (Provisional) on 1 February 1966. The 3960th SW inactivated on 1 April 1970, passing its other responsibilities to the 43rd SW, which formed that same day.

4133rd Bombardment Wing (Provisional)

The 4133rd BW (Provisional) took over responsibility for the TDY B-52 aircraft and crews at Andersen AFB, Guam, from the 3960th SW on 1 February 1966, and performed this role until 1 July 1970, when the 43rd SW took over.

4252nd Strategic Wing

The 4252nd SW at Kadena AB, Okinawa, had been activated on 1 December 1965. The wing may have exercised operational control over the B-52Ds deployed to Kadena under Operation Port Bow in February 1968. It was inactivated on 1 April 1970, being replaced by the 376th SW.

4258th SW

The 4258th SW was activated at U-Tapao on 2 June 1966 to control TDY tanker aircraft and aircrew. It may have exercised operational control over the B-52Ds deployed to U-Tapao from April 1967, although the base was initially used as a FOL only by Andersen-based aircraft, and did not become a fully autonomous base until January 1969. The 4258th SW inactivated on 1 April 1970, being replaced by the 307th SW.

APPENDIX F

B-52D/F NOSE-ART AND NAMES

B-52D

55-0061 *Big Country Bomber*, 337th BS/96th SAW, *Giant Voice '71*
55-0066 *City of Wichita Falls*
55-0067 *Lone Star Lady*
55-0067 *City of Fort Worth*, 20th BS/7th BW, *Giant Voice '74*
55-0071 *Calamity Jane*
55-0072 *City of Austin* and *City of Orlando*
55-0083 *Diamond Lil*
55-0086 *What's Tapioca*
55-0092 Sharkmouths, 43rd BW
55-0103 *Happiness is My Home*
55-0111 *Miss Patty J*
55-0112 *Larson's Lucky Lady*
56-0581 *Spokane, City of Lilac*
56-0582 Sharkmouths, 43rd SW
56-0589 *City of Burkburnett*
56-0591 *Tommy's Tigator*
56-0600 *Nighthawk*
56-0604 *East to Westover*
56-0619 *First Lady of Glasgow*, 99th BW
56-0620 *Maverick* and *Deterrent II*
56-0658 *Cong Crusher*
56-0666 *The Beast*
56-0672 *Night Missions . . . Blogh*
56-0675 *The Lavender Panther*, 325th BS/92nd BW, *Giant Voice '70*
56-0677 *City of Fort Worth*, *Clyde* and Sharkmouths, 43rd SW
56-0679 *Yellow Rose*
56-0680 *Orlando, Where the Action Is*, 367th BS/306th BW, *Giant Voice '71*
56-0692 *Lone Star*
56-0695 *Early Riser*

B-52F

57-0034 *Parker's Pride*
57-0042 *Hot Stuff*
57-0054 *Miss Magnolia*
57-0058 *Suzie Q*
57-0072 *That's All Folks*
57-0139 *Lady Luck*
57-0142 *Chain of Thunder*
57-0144 *Mekong Express*, 454th and 320th BWs
57-0152 *Casper the Friendly Ghost*, 320th BW
57-0163 *City of Sacramento*
57-0169 *Connie's Competition*
57-0169 *Thunder Express*, 320th BW

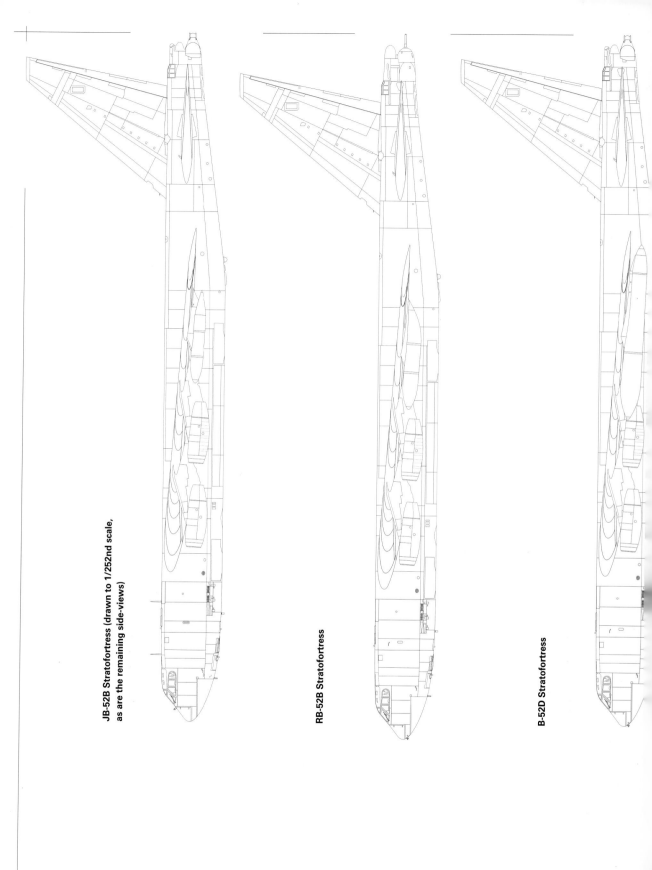

JB-52B Stratofortress (drawn to 1/252nd scale, as are the remaining side-views)

RB-52B Stratofortress

B-52D Stratofortress

B-52F Stratofortress

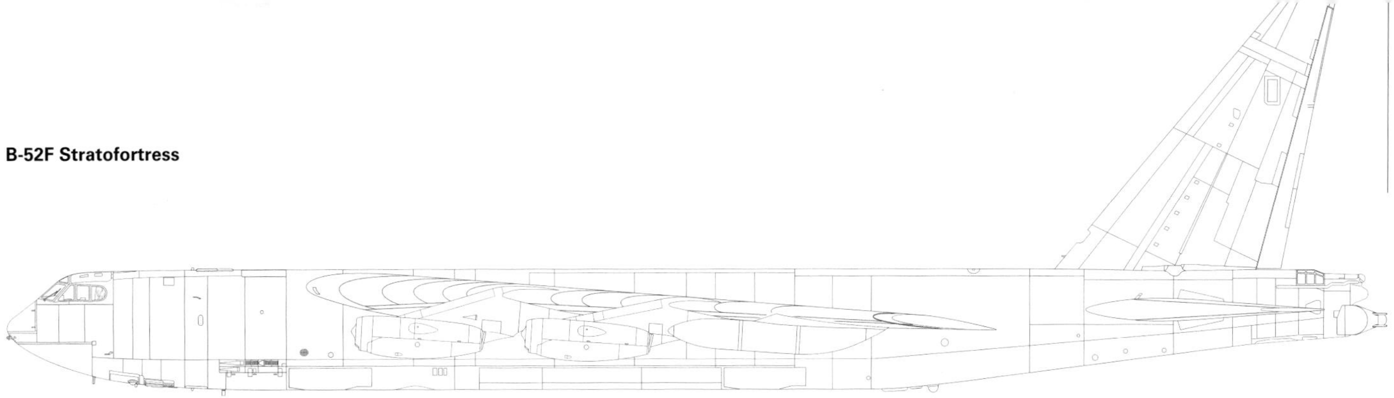

B-52G Stratofortress

B-52H Stratofortress

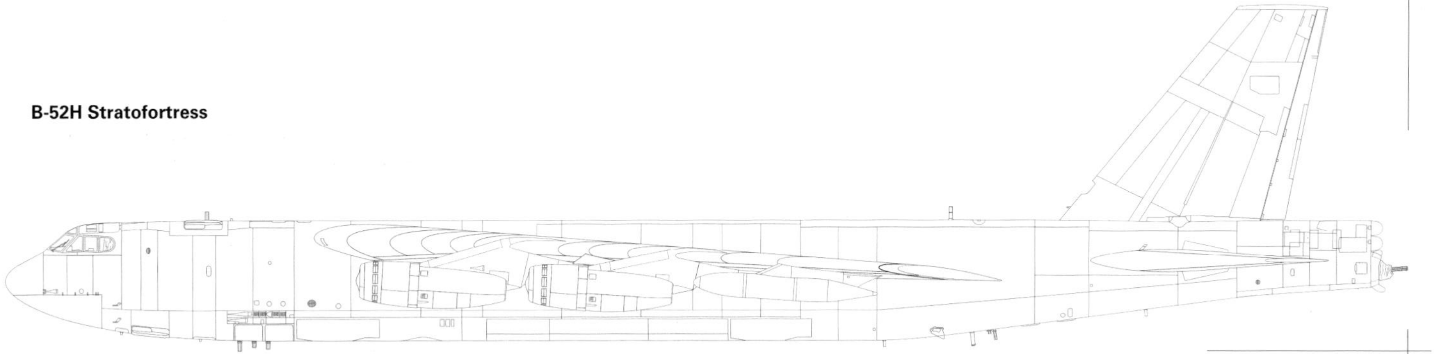

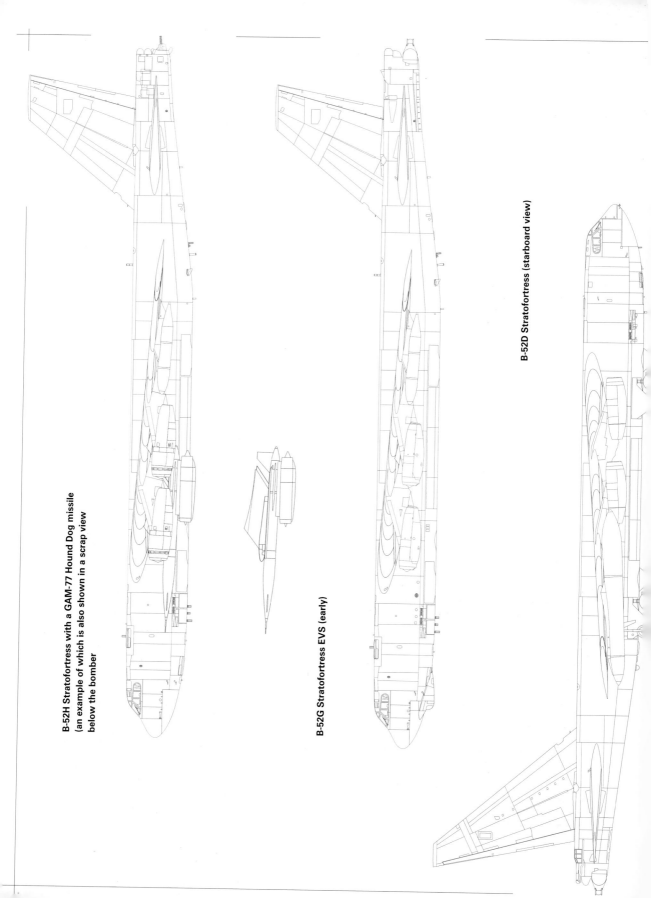

B-52H Stratofortress with a GAM-77 Hound Dog missile
(an example of which is also shown in a scrap view
below the bomber

B-52G Stratofortress EVS (early)

B-52D Stratofortress (starboard view)

COLOUR PLATES

1
JB-52B-5-BO 52-004, AFFTC, Edwards AFB, Operation *Redwing*, 1956

The B-52 formed the backbone of the USAF's SAC during the H-bomb era, and appropriately enough was also used in the final stages of the development of this awesome new weapon. *The Tender Trap* was the B-52 used for weapon effects studies during trials of the USA's new hydrogen bomb at Eniwetok, in the Marshall Islands. The aircraft flew close to a number of explosions, including two bombs dropped by another B-52, and was subsequently minutely inspected for the signs of blast, heat and radiation damage. Flown by one Maj C R Townsend, the aircraft was decorated with a pair of lip-sticked lips, in addition to its name. Legend has it that following the five test drops, the amorous Townsend was met on his return to Boeing Field by a beautiful woman, who stepped from a black limousine with a champagne bottle and two glasses! The aircraft later had its nose radome painted white and a pair of eyes added to the nose. Unusually, the bomber carried 1000-US gal underwing fuel tanks. The 'last four' of the serial was carried unhyphenated on the tailfin. Like most of the first batch of B-52Bs, 52-004 was fitted with the original tail turret, incorporating an A-3A fire control system and a quartet of 0.50-cal machine guns.

2
RB-52B-25-BO 53-0370, 93rd BW (Heavy), Castle AFB, 1957

Some 27 of the 50 B-52Bs built were dual role reconnaissance bombers, designated as RB-52Bs. This RB-52B is unusual in carrying the original small UNITED STATES AIR FORCE legend on its forward fuselage, since this had been officially superseded by the much larger U.S. AIR FORCE titling in 1955. It does, however, have the anti-flash white undersides, which were designed to reflect heat energy from an atomic explosion. The first B-52s entered service in natural metal finish, but they soon received anti-erosion silver FS 17178 aluminised acrylic nitro-cellulose paint on the uppersurfaces, with light grey paint on the rear parts of the engine nacelles. Anti-flash white undersurfaces (with a top-coat of FS 17875 white polyurethane) were added from 1956. Lettering was initially applied in the same 'Strata Blue' (FS 15045) colour as the SAC sash. A reconnaissance-capable RB-52B, this aircraft had a B-47 type M24-A-1 tail turret with twin 20 mm cannon and an MD-5 fire control system, the latter being housed in a larger, and more bulbous, aft-facing radome. When used in the reconnaissance role, the RB-52B carried a pressurised pod in the bomb-bay, accommodating cameras, mapping radars or ELINT sensors, as well as two dedicated crewmen, with a different capsule for photo-reconnaissance,

weather reconnaissance and ELINT. The aircraft also carried 24 M-120 photoflash bombs when configured for the photo-reconnaissance mission. The RB-52 boasts red wingtips, and has a red horizontal stripe on the tailfin – markings associated with the 93rd BW (Heavy), which was SAC's very first B-52 wing. The serial number was abbreviated to 3370 on the tailfin. This aircraft was finally retired to the Military Aircraft Storage and Disposal Center (MASDC) at Davis-Monthan AFB, Arizona, on 26 January 1966.

3
B-52H-140-BW 60-0021, 19th BW, Wurtsmith AFB, Cuban Missile Crisis, 1962

Although SAC aircraft rarely wore nose-art, this Hound Dog-armed B-52H bore a badge and two names (*Guardian of the Golden Peace* below the shield and *Homestead's Hesperides* behind it) at the time of the Cuban Missile Crisis. The 19th BW was then a brand new unit, having formed at Homestead in February 1962. The aircraft is armed with a pair of Douglas GAM-77 (later AGM-28) Hound Dog cruise missiles, each with a one megaton B28 nuclear warhead. These were powered by a 7500-lb st J52 turbojet engine, giving the missiles a stand-off range in excess of 600 miles and a speed of more than Mach 2. B-52 crews liked the Hound Dog, as its motor could be used to provide extra thrust on take-off. The missiles' fuel tanks would then be topped off from those of the carrier aircraft, which could itself be refuelled in flight. At this early stage of the B-52H's career, the bomber still lacked the white-topped cockpit, which was added to keep the crew compartment cool and to protect against atomic 'flash'. It also has its anti-flash white undersides extending over the bottoms of the intake cowls, which on later aircraft remained in silver finish. This B-52 carried most of its serial (00021) on the fin, with the 'last three' repeated on the nose. 60-0021 was later converted to launch the D-21 reconnaissance drone as part of the *Senior Crown* programme, and today remains in service as an attrition 'spare' with the 5th BW at Minot AFB. It has recently carried the name *Iron Eagle*, having previously been nicknamed *Black Jack*.

4
RB-52B-15-BO 52-8714, 22nd BW (Heavy), March AFB, March 1964

With an 'O-for-Obsolete' serial prefix indicating that it was ten years old, 52-8714 CITY OF *Riverside* became the first B-52 to be retired by SAC, going to Technical Training Command at Chanute AFB, Illinois on 8 March 1964. The rest of the 22nd, 93rd and 95th BWs' B-52Bs and RB-52Bs were retired from May 1965, the 95th subsequently deactivating and the other units re-equipping with later versions of the 'Buff'. The early Stratofortresses were held in storage at Davis-Monthan AFB for many years, before eventually being scrapped in accordance with strategic arms limitation treaties. This aircraft's anti-flash white undersides extended all over the engine nacelles, and the bomber also had a white top to the cockpit and forward fuselage. The serial 0-28714 was carried on the fin, with the 'last four' on the nose between the upper and lower radomes.

5
RB-52B-25-BO 53-0367, 22nd BW (Heavy), *Air Mail* reflex alert deployment, Andersen AFB, Guam, 1964

The long range of the B-52 largely freed it from the need to stand *Reflex Action* alert duties at overseas bases in the way in which the B-47 had done. *Reflex Action* procedures had replaced the earlier deployments that had seen entire Stratojet wings sent en masse to bases in North Africa and England (closer to their wartime targets), with 45 or so bombers supported by 20 KC-97 tankers. Under *Reflex Action* procedures, smaller numbers of aircraft were deployed to spend three weeks 'cocked' on nuclear-armed alert duty. The only B-52s to mount similar overseas alert duties were the B-52Bs of the 22nd and 95th BWs, which took over the *Air Mail* tasking previously carried out by B-47s at Andersen AFB, Guam, from April 1964 until mid-1965. This aircraft had a white top to its cockpit and forward fuselage, but did not have the white-painted rear fuselage forward of the tail unit. 53-0367 also had the twin 20 mm tail turret usually associated with the RB-52B. Unusually, the 030367 serial on the tailfin was not hyphenated, and the aircraft still had the original black/brown upper radome. Other early B-models had seen their radomes painted a lighter colour that matched the lower nose radome. The 'last four' was carried between the radomes, at the extreme nose. This aircraft was finally retired to MASDC on 6 January 1966.

6
B-52F-65-BW 57-0044, 3960th SW, Andersen AFB, Guam, July 1965

By the time it arrived at MASDC for storage, B-52F 57-0044 had a bomb-log recording 30 operational *Arc Light* missions over South Vietnam. The first two mission markers had small stars below the nose of each bomb. The aircraft wore its 'last four' (0044) in black well forward on the nose, between the upper and lower radomes, and the serial 70044 on the tailfin. The 'last four' was overpainted further back under the *U.S. AIR FORCE* titling. The SAC badge on the port nose was superimposed on the thicker version of the 'Milky Way' band. This aircraft had served with the 2nd BW at Barksdale and with the 320th BW at Mather AFB, before going to Southeast Asia with the 441st BS/320th BW between February and July 1965. The veteran bomber ended its operational career with the 93rd BW at Castle AFB, before being retired to MASDC on 28 January 1967.

7
B-52F-70-BW 57-0163, 3960th SW, Andersen AFB, Guam, 1965

57-0163 had been the first B-52 to be delivered to Mather AFB, arriving there on 4 October 1958. Soon christened *City of Sacramento*, it subsequently served with the 7th BW at Carswell, whose 9th and 20th BSs deployed to Guam during the second half of 1965. By the time the aircraft was in service with the 3960th SW, no trace of its name was visible, the bomber's 'last four' being applied in dayglo below the *U.S. AIR FORCE* legend, while 70163 was painted onto the tailfin. The aircraft was fitted with the later style pale grey upper nose radome, which matched the lower radome. The *City of Sacramento* had flown 30 *Arc Light* missions by the time it returned to the USA, and its original owners, the 320th BW, in 1965. Serving for a further four years, 57-0163 was eventually retired to MASDC on 2 July 1969.

8
B-52F-70-BW 57-0181, 3960th SW, Andersen AFB, Guam, late 1965

A veteran of an RAF Bombing Competition, the 7th BW's 57-0181 carried a white-outlined red '2' on its tailfin, denoting its previous use by the Second Air Force team – it also had a sprayed-out squadron badge on the tail above the '2'. Unit markings (apart from a wing badge to starboard, mirroring the SAC shield on the port side of the nose) were then extremely rare on SAC aeroplanes. During its stint on *Arc Light* operations, 57-0181 received the black undersides which were intended to reduce conspicuity during high altitude operations – these were introduced from about October 1965. Protection against atomic flash was clearly unnecessary in the Vietnam context. The aircraft was eventually retired to MASDC on 29 June 1967, and was subsequently transferred to Boeing's Wichita plant. Here, it was tested to destruction as part of the effort to assess, and extend, the structural life of SAC's remaining B-52Ds.

9
B-52F-65-BW 57-0149, 3960th SW, Andersen AFB, Guam, 1966

This B-52F was the aircraft flown by USAF Reserve Brig Gen Jimmy Stewart, better known as one of Hollywood's all time 'screen greats', during his inspection tour of Southeast Asia. Stewart had enjoyed a distinguished wartime career flying B-24s, but even after resuming his acting career he continued to take his Air Force Reserve duties extremely seriously. Stewart flew 57-0149 on a daylight bombing mission against VC infiltrators, marking the aircraft's 36th operation. The aircraft is unusual in employing the short underwing pylons, instead of the more common converted Hound Dog missile pylons. The bomber also wore its 'last four' in black on the nose between the radomes, and the 'last three' further aft in dayglo orange. After returning from Southeast Asia, 57-0149 was subsequently lost when it crashed just short of the runway at Castle AFB on 8 May 1969 and burned out.

10

B-52F-65-BW 57-0139, 3960th SW, Andersen AFB, Guam, 1966

Lady Luck from the 454th BW was the first B-52 to clock-up 100 missions in Vietnam, and it carried an impressive 'bomb log' on its nose. Names on B-52Fs were usually chosen and applied by the groundcrews, who spent longer with their individual aircraft than the TDY aircrews. Other examples included *Parker's Pride* (57-0034), *Hot Stuff* (57-0042), *Miss Magnolia* (57-0054), *Suzie Q* (57-0058), *That's All Folks* (57-0072), *Chain of Thunder* (57-0142) and *Connie's Competition* (57-0164). *Lady Luck's* black undersides had been quite crudely applied, with evidence of overspray onto the uppersurface silver. The aircraft wore the serial 70139 on the tail, with the 'last four' in black on the nose below and behind the cockpit. The bomber was eventually retired to the MASDC 'boneyard' on 30 May 1973.

11

B-52F-65-BW 57-0144, 3960th SW, Andersen AFB, Guam, 1966

The *Mekong Express* was one of the most successful of the 320th BW's B-52Fs deployed to Southeast Asia, flying its 22nd mission in October 1965, and eventually logging 86 *Arc Light* sorties. Although the black undersides applied to these aircraft covered the original anti-flash white, the precise demarcation differed from aircraft to aircraft. The trailing edge of 57-0144's rudder was noticeably darker than the tailfin, making it appear black in some contemporary black and white photographs. The aircraft carried the serial 70144 on the tail, with the 'last four' on the nose, in black. The 441st BS's *Mekong Express* was the subject of a series of PR photos, at least one of which was still in official use (on leaflets dropped on Taliban positions) in 2002 – 35 years after they were taken! The Stratofortress served with the 320th BW before being deployed to Southeast Asia, and then briefly with the 454th BW upon its return to the USA. It was retired to MASDC soon after its tour of combat in Southeast Asia, entering the 'boneyard' in November 1967.

12

B-52F-65-BW 57-0152, 3960th SW, Andersen AFB, Guam, 1966

The black undersurfaces on 57-0152 were particularly neatly applied, with little overspray. The aircraft dropped the B-52's 50,000th bomb in Vietnam, during the course of its 29th mission. It was known as 'Casper the Friendly Ghost', although this name was not carried. Instead, the aircraft had only a small representation of the cartoon character in white, sprayed onto its nose immediately below the *S.* in *U.S. AIR FORCE*. 57-0152 was finally sent into retirement at MASDC on 18 August 1971.

13

B-52F-70-BW 57-0169, 3960th SW, Andersen AFB, Guam, 1967

Thunder Express carried 68 mission marks when it returned from Southeast Asia, 57-0169 being one of the USAF's longest serving B-52Fs. Indeed, it remained with the 93rd BW at Castle AFB for crew training after the withdrawal of the F-model from the frontline in 1971. The aircraft was eventually retired to MASDC on 20 October 1978, by which time it was one of the last B-52Fs still in service with the Air Force.

14

B-52H-175-BW 61-0035, 46th BS/319th BW, Grand Forks AFB, July 1968

While the B-52Fs became increasingly committed to the escalating conflict in Southeast Asia, CONUS-based B-52G/H units continued to stand alert and practice their deadly deterrent missions. In 1968, these aircraft still mostly wore the original silver and white colour scheme, although the shift to low-level penetration tactics had led to the gradual adoption of camouflage. This B-52H has a white top to the forward fuselage, protecting the cockpit and avionics compartments from excessive heat, and also has the whole rear fuselage (but not the tail) painted white. 61-0035 remains in service today as an attrition reserve aircraft with the 5th BW at Minot. Names worn by the bomber over the decades include *Freebird*.

15

B-52D-60-BO 55-0101, 4133rd BW, Andersen AFB, Guam, 1968

Before being sent for service in South East Asia, B-52Ds were camouflaged (to T.O.1-1-4 specifications) with black (FS 17038 or 27038) undersides and a set pattern of dark green (FS 34079), blue green (FS 34159) and tan (FS 24201 or 34201) on the uppersurfaces. The anti-dazzle panel in front of the windscreen remained in matt black. Unit markings were omitted, and the aircraft serial number was applied on the tailfin in red (FS 11136). Some aircraft had the last four digits (sometimes the second digit of the FY prefix plus the last three) of the serial repeated on the nose, while others had the 'last three' only. Positioning of this varied, with some aircraft having it applied in red and others in white – sometimes in white reflective tape. Most aircraft in Vietnam had a white reflective stripe applied to the underwing tanks, often with the 'last three' superimposed. While many B-52Fs deployed for operations over Vietnam carried bomb log type mission tallies, relatively few B-52Ds wore them. 55-0101 was an exception, boasting 30 red mission marks on the port side of the nose in 1968. Unusually, the aircraft had the code 0101 in red on the extreme nose, between the upper and lower radomes. On the starboard side, 101 had been applied in white reflective tape on top of the red number, but this had eroded off the port side. The aircraft was decorated with a white reflective tank stripe, with the 'last three' superimposed. Due to the aircraft being more than ten years old, the ageing B52 was marked with the 'O-for-Obsolete' serial prefix on the tail, this being presented as 0-50101.The aircraft carried short pylons. Having completed a quarter-century of frontline service, 55-0101 was finally retired to the 'boneyard' on 6 October 1982.

16

B-52D-80-BO 56-0629, 4258th SW, U-Tapao, 1968
56-0629 was the penultimate Seattle-built B-52D, being delivered to the USAF in October 1957. Eleven years later, the ageing aircraft was fighting hard in Vietnam, and was extremely badly weathered and in urgent need of a visit to the paint shop. The original silver paint showed through on the nose and on the converted Hound Dog pylons, as well as on the fin leading edge. Some traces of the *U.S. AIR FORCE* legend even seemed to be showing through the black paint on the nose. The last three digits of the serial were applied in white on the nose, between the upper and lower radomes. The 'Buff' also boasted an 'O-for-Obsolete' serial prefix on the fin due to its age. At roughly 1609Z on 26 December 1972, while flying at 37,000 ft over Duc Noi, 56-0629 (callsign 'Black 03') was hit by ground fire, but returned safely to U-Tapao. The 14 external holes and three dents took some 63 man hours to repair, and the aircraft returned to service on New Year's Eve 1972. From 1967, B-52Ds assigned to combat missions in Southeast Asia gained a series of electronic warfare upgrades under the *Rivet Rambler* or Phase V ECM programme. In the high threat environment encountered over Vietnam, the aircraft received a number of warning receivers, including a single AN/ALR-18 automated set-on receiving set, an AN/ALR-20 panoramic receiver set and an AN/APR-25 radar homing and warning system. Modified B-52Ds were also fitted with six AN/ALE-20 flare dispensers (with 96 IR decoy flares) and eight AN/ALE-24 chaff dispensers (with 1125 chaff bundles). They also received a comprehensive jamming suite, with four AN/ALT-6B or AN/ALT-22 continuous wave jamming transmitters, two AN/ALT-16 barrage-jamming systems and two AN/ALT-32H and one AN/ALT-32L high- and low-band jamming sets. This aircraft was duly preserved at Barksdale AFB following its retirement, the combat veteran now sporting an impressive bomb log recording its operational career over Vietnam.

17

B-52D-35-BW 56-0678, 4258th SW, U-Tapao, February 1969
56-0678 was another B-52D damaged during *Linebacker II*, the aircraft (callsign 'Lilac 03') being hit on 18 December 1972, but landing safely at U-Tapao. Although there was no in-spar damage, 24 areas required repair kits, and no fewer than 350 external holes were patched or repaired. After 60,000 man hours the aircraft was finally restored to airworthy status on 30 July 1973. It carried its

'last four' on the nose below the cockpit in red. In 1969 the aircraft had the usual white tank stripe and 'last three', and also used the older short pylon. No O- serial prefix was carried. This long-serving B-52D was retired to AMARC on either 12 or 17 October 1978.

18

B-52D-65-BO 55-0105, 4258th SW, U-Tapao February 1969
55-0105 was a Seattle-built B-52D which saw extensive service in Southeast Asia. It is depicted here carrying a 21-mission bomb log made up of stencilled red bombs. Unusually, the aircraft did not carry its 'last three' or 'last four' on the nose. The bomber had the usual white tank stripe, flanking the 'last four' (5105) – this was not a standard marking. 55-0105 was fitted with the older short pylons. No O- serial prefix was carried. This B-52D was the penultimate D-model to be retired to AMARC, arriving there just before 56-0674 in early October 1983 following service with the 96th BW at Dyess. The bomber subsequently went to Seoul, in South Korea, where it was put on display.

19

B-52D-25-BW 55-0677, 43rd BW, Andersen AFB, Guam, 1972
A number of the 43rd BW's aircraft were adorned with sharksmouths from late 1972 onwards, the first being so-decorated with the permission of the then wing CO Col (later Brigadier General) James McCarthy. This aircraft was B-52D 55-0677, which wore a huge sharksmouth on the nose, and whose serial was carried as 50677, without the old O-prefix for a ten-year-old aeroplane. 56-0582 is often said to have been similarly marked. By the time it reached the 'boneyard', the wing's 55-0092 carried a much smaller sharkmouth insignia, with white teeth and a black and red mouth, but this was believed to date from after the Vietnam War. 55-0677, by contrast, participated in *Linebacker II* during December 1972, wearing these gaudy markings and carrying 750-lb bombs on the short pylons. Some reports describe the 43rd BW's shark-mouthed B-52 as being 56-0677, but this latter aircraft had already been lost, on 30 July 1972, after a lightning strike knocked out its instruments and it crashed in Thailand en route back to U-Tapao. In September 1970, units in Southeast Asia received a technical directive requiring aircraft to be repainted with polyurethane paint, which proved much more resilient, and in the later years of the war, camouflaged B-52s lost their sometimes peeling, patchy and matted appearance.

20

B-52D-30-BW 56-0658, 307th SW, U-Tapao, 3 December 1973
56-0658 remained at U-Tapao after *Linebacker II*, and was still flying training missions (fully armed with 750-lb bombs) at the end of 1973. On 3 December 1973, the 'Buff' was flown by Capt Wright and Crew E09 from Carswell as 'Gold 02',

together with two other B-52Ds. The formation leader was 'Gold 01' (56-0695), a 'Pave' 'Buff' leadship now preserved at Tinker AFB. 56-0658 wore the SAC badge just aft of the cockpit to port, but no matching wing badge was applied on the other side. The 'last three' was painted on in red on the nose below the cockpit, but not on the tank stripe. This aircraft was retired to AMARC on 29 April 1982. For some of its career, the bomber was marked with the name *Cong Crusher*.

21

B-52D-25-BW 55-0677 *City of FORT WORTH*, 7th BW, Carswell AFB, Texas, 1974
Also the subject of profile 19, 55-0677 survived the war and went on to join the Carswell-based 20th BS, which was part of the 7th BW. It represented the wing in the 1974 *Giant Voice* bombing competition, wearing a massive yellow winged '2' on the tailfin (indicating its allocation to the Second Air Force team) and the name *City of FORT WORTH* on the nose. The 'last three' was presented in yellow. This has commonly been reported on B-52Ds, but was usually a misinterpretation of a faded red 'last three' or a yellowed 'last three' originally painted on in white. Despite its age, the aircraft carried no 'O-for-Obsolete' serial prefix, instead having 50677 applied to the tailfin. *City of FORT WORTH* wore the SAC emblem on the port side of the nose and a 7th Bomb Wing emblem on the starboard side. The aircraft was finally retired to the Yankee Air Museum at Ypsilanti, Michigan. Today, it wears an approximation of its *Linebacker* colour scheme, albeit with a very gaudy, three-dimensional and more detailed sharksmouth than was originally applied.

22

B-52D-35-BW 56-0676, 22nd BW, Beale AFB, 1980
Following active service in Southeast Asia, 56-0676 enjoyed a long career with the 22nd BW, the 43rd SW at Andersen AFB and finally the 92nd BW at Fairchild. The aircraft, seen here with GBU-15 glide bombs and with its serial applied simply as 60676, was actually the last active D-model when it was retired on 1 October 1983, although 56-0674 made its last flight (ferrying to Davis-Monthan) three days later. 56-0676 (by then back with the 43rd SW at Andersen AFB) was flown out of Guam by the 43rd's CO, Col Dudley M Moorhous, who had been the first man to clock up 300 combat missions in the B-52D. The aircraft was subsequently preserved at Fairchild AFB, Washington. Today, it remains a part of the base museum, in company with a B-26, a B-52G and a C-47, as well as examples of the F-101, F-105, T-33 and T-37. While serving with the 307th SW at U-Tapao, this aircraft (callsign 'Brown 03') participated in *Linebacker II*, and on the opening night of the campaign (18 December 1972) was a part of the first wave of 48 B-52s, which comprised 21 B-52Ds from U-Tapao and 12 B-52Ds and 15 B-52Gs from Andersen. These reached their targets at 1945 hrs local Hanoi time. Wave One reached its first targets

just as 'Snow' cell dropped 324 bombs onto the runway at Hao Lac airfield, on the south-western edge of Hanoi. 56-0676's tail gunner, S/Sgt Samuel O Turner, downed an attacking MiG-21 during the course of the mission – the first air-to-air kill in the B-52's combat history. Turner won the Silver Star for his feat. Five more MiGs were claimed by B-52 tail gunners during *Linebacker II*, but only one of these was actually confirmed – on 24 December A1C Albert Moore downed a second MiG-21 during a mission against the Thai Nguyen railway yard. Interestingly, Moore's MiG-killing B-52D is also preserved, with a red star kill marking and a post-war bomb log, at the USAF Academy at Colorado Springs.

23

B-52G-90-BW 57-6516, 63rd BS (Provisional)/72nd SW (Provisional), Andersen AFB, Guam, 1972
Although newer than the B-52Ds, the B-52Gs deployed to Andersen lacked the older aircraft's massive bombload and upgraded ECM equipment. They were therefore assigned to the less challenging targets attacked during *Linebacker*. This aircraft was deployed to Southeast Asia from the 455th BW at Beale AFB, California, leaving its base on 15 April 1972. The bomber wore the standard SIOP colour scheme, with the same dark green (FS 34079), blue green (FS 34159) and tan (FS 24201 or 34201) camouflage as the B-52D on the uppersurfaces, but extending over the tailfin, nose and fuselage sides, with anti-flash white undersides. Aircraft sent to Southeast Asia as part of the *Bullet Shot* deployments wore white or yellow tank stripes, but without the 'last three' digits of the serial number superimposed. This 'Buff' carries most of its serial (76516) and the *USAF* legend on the fin-top in black, with the 'last four' repeated under the cockpit. SAC and wing markings were not applied. 57-6516 was retired to the 'boneyard' on 8 October 1991, having flown 12 missions in *Desert Storm* as *Ultimate Warrior*.

24

B-52G-100-BW 58-0201, 72nd SW (Provisional), Andersen AFB, Guam, 1972
Unusually, this B-52G wore a SAC shield below the cockpit and its 'last four' in yellow on the forward fuselage, although well aft of the cockpit. The aircraft also had a white nose radome, and the upper part was unpainted. These features were unusual on B-52Gs used in Southeast Asia. Following the establishment of the 63rd BS (Provisional), further B-52Gs that had deployed to Guam formed the 72nd SW (Provisional), which in turn controlled the 64th, 65th and 486th BSs (Provisional). 58-0201, operating as 'Charcoal 01', was lost on the night of 18 December 1972 during the first *Linebacker II* mission. The aircraft was being flown by a 340th BS/ 97th BW crew who had been scheduled to be returning to Blytheville aboard a KC -135, but their replacements had been late getting to Guam due to heavy snows at their Loring base. The aircraft was hit by two SA-2 SAMs over Yen Vien Railway Yard,

and only Radar Navigator Maj Richard Johnson, Navigator Capt Robert Certain and EWO Capt Richard Simpson escaped. The pilot, Lt Col Donald Rissi, co-pilot 1Lt Robert Thomas and gunner E7 Walter Ferguson went down with the aircraft, and their bodies were later returned to the USA by the Vietnamese government.

25

B-52G-110-BW 58-0244, 72nd SW (Provisional), Andersen AFB, Guam, 1972

58-0244 was possibly one of the few B-52Gs to sortie with an AN/ALQ-119 ECM pod underwing during the *Linebacker II* operation. Only a handful were employed, and it cannot be ascertained for certain whether 58-0244 was one of the aircraft so-equipped. The bomber lacked wing and SAC badges and carried its 'last four' in black on the nose. Later named *Hellsadroppin*, 58-0244 was finally retired to the 'boneyard' on 29 October 1991.

26

B-52H-140 60-0021, 4200th SS, Beale AFB, 1970

Two H-model 'Buffs' (B-52H-140-BW 60-0021 and B-52H-150-BW 60-0036) were converted to carry the D-21B reconnaissance drone under Operation *Senior Bowl*, funded by the CIA. The D-21 had originally been designed for launch from the trisonic Lockheed A-12 (developed alongside the SR-71), but difficulties (culminating in a fatal accident) forced Lockheed to find a new carrier. The D-21 drone was modified to D-21B standards, with a 90-second solid fuel rocket booster for accelerating the drone to its 80,000 ft operating altitude and Mach 3 operating speed. The first of the two launch aircraft (B-52H-140-BW 60-0021) was sent to Palmdale on 12 December 1966, where it was fitted with massive inboard underwing pylons from which the D-21s could be suspended. The gunner and EWO positions in the cockpit were also replaced by new Launch Control Officer stations. The aircraft were fitted with camera ports in the fuselage sides and in the launch pylons to allow the launch to be filmed, but the normal tail armament was retained, contrary to some reports. After training at Groom Lake ('The Ranch') with a unit simply known as A Flight, the two D-21 carriers were operated from late 1968 by the 4200th Support Squadron (SS) at Beale, being kept on a virtual alert status with two 'birds' on each B-52H. After launch from Beale, the B-52Hs flew to Andersen, Hickam or Kadena AFBs, from where operational missions were mounted. Sorties were flown on 9 November 1969, 16 December 1970, 4 March 1971 and 20 March 1971. The first and last drones were lost over enemy territory, and the second and third missions were fruitless because the vital palletised camera hatches containing the mission film were not recovered after being ejected from the drones. All the D-21Bs launched from 4200th SS B-52Hs were dropped from the starboard pylon, with the port station carrying the back-up D-21B, which was never used operation-

ally. The programme was terminated on 23 July 1971. The aircraft wore standard early style SIOP camouflage, with painted radomes, although 60-0036 featured a non-standard white-painted cockpit roof to reflect the bright sun at high altitude. Both 'Buffs' remain operational today, having served as attrition reserve aircraft with the 5th BW's 23rd BS at Minot AFB during the late 1990s. 60-0021 (depicted earlier in its career in profile 3) still serves with the 23rd BS, while 60-0036 was transferred from the 72nd BS at Minot to Edwards AFB in July 2002. The latter jet still wears its *Tagboard Flyer* nose art.

27

B-52F-65-BW 57-0148, 329th BS/93rd BW, Castle AFB, California, 1971

A relatively small number of B-52Fs (perhaps as few as 28 aircraft), together with a handful of B-52C/Es, received the later SIOP camouflage scheme. These aircraft were generally those which remained operational with the Hound Dog missile, as the older 'tall-tail' variants used in the training role typically retained their original silver finish. Unusually, this aircraft had the *USAF* legend and serial 57148 applied in 'stencil' style on the tailfin, while the 'Winged 2' badge was added for a 1971 bombing competition. 57-0148 was finally retired to the 'boneyard' on 15 August 1978.

28

B-52G-95-BW 58-0174, 456th BW, Beale AFB, California, December 1973

Although B-52s still remained ready for further action in Vietnam as 1973 drew to a close, Stateside B-52 units continued to stand alert as part of the USA's Cold War defence posture. Carrying Hound Dog missiles underwing, 58-0174 had the later white nose radome normally associated (on camouflaged aeroplanes) with 'Buffs' that had received EVS and Phase VI EW improvements. A white nose without the 'lumps and bumps' that were synonymous with these modifications was never common. In 1973, wing badges were rare, and even the SAC badge itself was not often applied. This aircraft was lost on 8 February 1974 after it suffered a series of multiple engine fires and failures whilst attempting to take off from Beale AFB.

29

B-52H-175-BW 61-0032, 17th BW, Wright Patterson AFB, Ohio, circa 1974

When the SRAM replaced the Hound Dog in SAC service, the alert B-52G/Hs still had smooth nose contours, lacking EVS sensor turrets and the ECM antennas added as part of *Rivet Rambler VI*. This B-52H wears the standard early SIOP colour scheme adopted when SAC moved over to low level tactics in the mid-1960s. Boeing's AGM-69A SRAM entered service with the 42nd BW in March 1972, the missile originally being carried in clusters of six (in tandem triples) on the underwing hardpoints. Internal carriage was adopted on Offensive

Avionics System-modified aircraft, however, these machines beginning to enter service in 1981. After that, SRAMs became an option for the Common Strategic Rotary Launcher, which was introduced from 1988. The weapon was withdrawn from the inventory in June 1990 following rocket motor leaks and other safety concerns. B-52H 61-0032 remains in frontline service, however, being used by AFRC's 917th Wing during Operation *Enduring Freedom* in late 2001 The veteran bomber flew a series of long range missions from the island of Diego Garcia, in the Indian Ocean, to Afghanistan, where it bombed Taliban targets. Two years earlier, 61-0032 had been displayed at the 1999 Royal International Air Tattoo at RAF Cottesmore, in Leicestershire.

30
B-52G-120-BW 59-2569, 28th BW, Ellsworth AFB, 1976

Most B-52G/Hs received the new EVS sensor turrets and Phase VI radomes together, and to see just the EVS FLIR and LLTV turrets below an otherwise unblemished original nose was uncommon. The original semi-painted nose radome was also uncommon on EVS-equipped aircraft, which generally received a new radome, characterised by external strips running fore and aft. This aircraft did have the array of AN/ALQ-155 blade antennas under the forward fuselage, however, these usually being associated with the Phase VI EW fit. This long-serving B-52G was finally retired to the 'boneyard' in February 1994.

BIBLIOGRAPHY

Boeing B-52 Stratofortress *by Peter E Davies and Tony Thornborough*, Crowood, 1998
B-52 Stratofortress – Boeing's Cold War Warrior *by Robert F Dorr and Lindsay Peacock*, Osprey, 1995
Boeing B-52 – A Documentary History *by Walter Boyne*, Jane's, 1981
B-52 Stratofortress *by Jeff Ethell and Joe Christy*, Ian Allan, 1981
B-52 – Ageing BUFFs Youthful Crews *by René J Francillon and Peter B Lewis*, Osprey, 1988
B-52 Stratofortress in action *by Larry Davis*, Squadron/Signal, 1992
Boeing B-52G/H Stratofortress – Aerofax Datagraph 7 *by D R Jenkins and B Rogers*, Aerofax, 1990
B-52 Stratofortress in detail and scale *by Alwyn T Lloyd*, Detail and Scale, 1988
B-52 Aeroguide 28 *by Anthony Thornborough*, Linewrights, 1990
B-52, *Przeglad Konstrukcii Lotniczych*, 1992
Walk Around B-52 Stratofortress *by Lou Drendel*, Squadron/Signal, 1996
Air War Hanoi *by Robert F Dorr*, Blandford, 1988
Air War South Vietnam *by Robert F Dorr*, Arms and Armour, 1990
Allied Aircraft Art *by John M and Donna Campbell*, Schiffer, 1992
Exterior Finishes, Insignia and Markings Applicable to USAF Aircraft and Missiles, USAF, 1961
Planes, Names and Dames, Vol III 1955-1975 *by Larry Davis*, Squadron/Signal, 1995
Shark's Teeth Nose Art *by Jeffrey L Ethell*, Motorbooks, 1992
Strategic Air Command *by Lindsay T Peacock*, 1988
Strategic Air Command Unit Mission and History Summaries, HQ SAC, 1988
USAF Strike Aircraft *by Joe Cupido*, Osprey, 1991
Vietnam – The Air War *by Robert F Dorr*, Osprey, 1991
Vietnam – Combat from the Cockpit, *Robert F Dorr*, Airlife, 1989

INDEX

References to illustrations are shown in **bold**. Plates are shown with page and caption locators in (brackets).